THE YOUNG REPUBLICANS

THE YOUNG REPUBLICANS

*A RECORD OF THE
WELSH REPUBLICAN MOVEMENT —
MUDIAD GWERINIAETHOL CYMRU*

by
'Gweriniaethwr'

GWASG Carreg Gwalch

Text © 'Gweriniaethwr' 1996

All rights reserved. No part of this publication may be reproduced or transmitted, in any form or by any means, without permission.

ISBN: 0-86381-362-3

First published in 1996 by Gwasg Carreg Gwalch, Iard yr Orsaf, Llanrwst, Gwynedd, Wales.
☎ (01492) 642031

Printed and published in Wales.

Cyflwynedig
i Eluned Rhys a'r Meibion
ac
i Mrs Lil Phillips (gynt o Birmingham) am ei chroeso
i bawb o Gymru.

Er cof amdani
ac
i'r rhai a safodd a'r rhai a saif
dros y Weriniaeth.

Rhagair/Foreword

"Gair i'n darllenwyr Cymraeg: Yn yr iaith fain yr ysgrifennir y rhan fwyaf o'r Bwletin hwn. Yn Saesneg hefyd y cynhelir y rhan fwyaf o weithgarwch y Mudiad. Nid yw hyn yn golygu diystyrrwch o werth ein hiaith fawreddog. Ond i holl genedl y Cymry y mae ein neges ni", ysgrifennodd Huw Davies yn Ionawr 1950 yn y *Bwletin*, newyddlen a gyhoeddwyd gan Fudiad Gweriniaethol Cymru (bu raid i fwy na hanner blwyddyn fynd heibio cyn i gyhoeddiad newyddiadurol mwy sylweddol y Mudiad, *The Welsh Republican — Y Gweriniaethwr*, ddechrau ymddangos).

Mae'r hanes hwn am weriniaethwyr Cymru yn ymestyn yn ôl o'r ganrif hon at weithgareddau a delfrydau ein cyndadau yn y ganrif o'r blaen. Y mae wedi'i sgrifennu yn Saesneg (ar wahân i ambell ddarn yn y Gymraeg o dudalennau *Y Gweriniaethwr* a'r Wasg Gymraeg) am y rheswm a gynigiodd Huw Davies bron hanner canrif yn ôl: At holl genedl y Cymry y mae pwysigrwydd neges hanfodol yr hanes hwn wedi ei anelu.

★ ★ ★

The aspiration, the burning conviction behind The Welsh Republican Movement — *Mudiad Gweriniaethol Cymru* when it came to take more formal shape in the mid-years of this present century was no new political phenomenon in the history of Wales. Many of our forefathers who took part in the rebellions of the 19th and earlier centuries died with the ideal of their country freed from the taint of alien imperial royalism alive in their minds. It is an ideal which has lived through the generations. And it is to the generation of today that we look to honour and make real at last those fierce dreams of our forbears, and in so doing help to set all Welsh men and women worthy of the name on the road of self-respect and national freedom again.

'Gweriniaethwr'
Ionawr 1996

Chapter 1

"Republicanism in Wales is the inheritor of the ideals of Glyndŵr as of 'Becca, of the martyrdom of Penderyn as of the Tonypandy miners . . . it is no new adaptation of a foreign creed . . . it is the traditional and age-old voice of Wales itself," wrote Ifor Huws Wilks, a young student of history and philosophy at Bangor University in 1951.

And how right he was. The truth in those words had been brought home to him with compelling conviction as a result of his researching into the history of the survival of our people through the centuries of English domination, and in particular that of the revolutionary movements of the Welsh working people in the 19th century rising in challenge to subjection and exploitation. At the time of their writing Republicanism in Wales had already come into formal political existence with the formation of the Welsh Republican Movement — Mudiad Gweriniaethol Cymru some two years earlier, and Wilks was writing in *The Welsh Republican — Y Gweriniaethwr*, the official publication of that Movement. A quote from a letter of his in 1952 soon after he had been made editor of *The Welsh Republican* adds force to his words:

> "Am getting a new slant on the Newport Rising of 1839! Apparently the general idea was to set up what was variously called a 'Chartist kingdom' or a 'Republic' in South Wales — to be maintained in its first stages by the blowing up of Newport Bridge and thus cutting off the usual flow of English troops from London, etc. by GWR to Bristol and then by march via Chepstow to Newport. Brecon, Newport and Monmouth were the three key positions to be taken to cover eastern approaches! Frost was a pawn, Chartism to a large extent a cover-movement; the real dynamism came from those who had risen, not unsuccessfully, in Merthyr in 1831, and who, following the collapse there, turned from the theory of the Rising to the theory of underground organisation (viz. The Scotch Cattle), and then finally turned to the theory of the Rising again.
>
> Prominent in the Newport affair was a certain Irishman who had escaped into Wales following the Irish Rebellion [which one is not specified] and who had also been associated with the Whiteboys."

But it was from the immediate post-war generation of Nationalist students at Aberystwyth University in the late 1940s that had come much of the impetus towards the eventual establishment of Republicanism as an effective means of carrying forward the fight for the freedom of their country. Prominent amongst them, as Chairman and Secretary respectively of the University branch of the Welsh Nationalist Party (now known as Plaid Cymru), were Gwilym Prys Davies and W. Huw R. Davies. Both of them had served in the Navy during the war, and their experience there, together with indications everywhere of the disintegration of the old imperial world order, had made them impatient of what they considered to be the Nationalist Party's timidity and over-emphasis on maintaining a strictly constitutionalist approach in setting its aim for Wales to be that of Dominion Status within the British Commonwealth of Nations. The two Davieses had soon come into contact with the redoubtable John Legonna in Aberystwyth, and through him with Trefor Morgan, both of whom had served short terms of imprisonment during the war years when they had come into political conflict with the wartime authorities, and who both were subsequently to play a part in the activities of the WRM.

In the Autumn of 1947 Cliff Bere published his pamphlet, *The Welsh Republic*. Bere was a member of the Caerdydd branch of the Welsh Nationalist Party. The publication of the pamphlet brought him for the first time into awareness of and contact with the restless elements of the Party in Aberystwyth, Abertawe, Bangor and elsewhere. Before long there was a nucleus of members in the Caerdydd branch itself who wished to bring the Republican issue forward for serious consideration in the formulation of Party policy. But they were not in sufficient strength to vote it onto the agenda of the Party Conference of 1948.

Under the Nationalist Party's constitution at that time six was the minimum number of members necessary for the formation of a new branch. The work of the Caerdydd branch was carried on almost exclusively in Welsh. So, with some misgiving, but perhaps with some element of justification too, as several of its members were not Welsh-speaking, it was decided to propose the formation of a so-called English-speaking branch in Caerdydd to work alongside the existing one. Whether or not those in authority in the Party fully appreciated all the possible implications attending the establishment of such a branch, it is not easy to know at this distance of time. However, the fact that they felt duly obliged to honour the constitutional rules of the Party and approve the new branch coming into existence, whatever any misgivings they themselves might have had, can only be seen as a tribute to their fairmindedness.

The branch was duly formed with a membership of very few more than six to begin. By now Huw Davies had come down from Aberystwyth to Caerdydd. And Trefor Morgan, living in Aberaman in the Cynon Valley, was never far away.

On the 23rd October 1948 a gathering of Republican-minded Nationalists from a wide spread of locations meeting in a room at the old Cory Hall in Queen Street Station approach, Caerdydd, saw the formation of a coherent body of politically motivated Republican opinion in Wales. From then on Republicanism became the theme of an increasing number of Nationalist meetings, more often than not held in the open air on the streets of the southern valley towns. In the Tawe Valley there are vivid memories still of the atmosphere and excitement of such meetings at, for instance, Clydach, Pontardawe and Ystalyfera, sometimes in the light of the street lamps after dusk had fallen, and often before audiences of as many as forty or fifty mainly appreciative listeners.

By the beginning of 1949 the Republican group was in contact with Ithel Davies, a barrister in Abertawe and a Nationalist of radical renown. In the Autumn of 1947 he had gone to Aberystwyth to address the University students at their invitation, and the flow of his humane and radical zeal had duly impressed more than one member of the group who had been there at the time. And so in February 1949 Ithel Davies was invited to draft an official statement of Republican policy. (This, after some little adjustment, was eventually to be published in Welsh and English as The Welsh Republican Manifesto, a Statement of Policy for The Welsh Republican Movement.)

In the meantime, however, Republican activities in the field, so to speak, were not being neglected. On the 30th April 1949 James Griffiths, Minister in the Labour government of the day, paid a visit to his home territory to address a meeting in Rhydaman (*Ammanford*). Republicans made it their business to attend that meeting. As had been stressed in *The Welsh Republic*, the policy of the Labour government of stubbornly opposing any measure of self-government for Wales was at one with that of the Tory Party, and Welsh-speaking Griffiths seemed to provide no exception to that imperial policy. This was a far cry from the time when the right of Wales and the other Celtic nations of Britain to self-government was a basic and boasted tenet of Labour Party policy.

The Republicans rose at intervals during the Rhydaman meeting to express their views. The Minister threw the charge of 'nationalist fascists' in the faces of his accusers, who, however, were well-qualified to shout in return — 'Call us what you will, James Griffiths — but it's we who fought Hitler'. The fact that the newspaper reports of the meeting referred to the interrupters as 'members of the Nationalist Party' suggests that the idea of Republican motivation behind the Nationalist cause had not yet gained recognition. But the young Republicans themselves had gained worthwhile experience there in the tactics of making their presence felt.

On the 9th of May a little more than a week after the Rhydaman meeting,

James Griffiths was back in his Llanelli constituency, and at a meeting there, referring to a 'recent attempt by young Nationalists to wreck a meeting at Rhydaman', he said: "It displayed a spirit of racial arrogance that was the nearest approach to the Hitler Youth Movement I have encountered in this country." It seemed that the young Republicans had made enough of an impact on James Griffiths for him to think it necessary for him to return at the earliest opportunity to try to impress on his constituents that his prior allegiance was after all to them in Wales and not to his English career. His slanderous racialist remarks were by now becoming part and parcel of his political repertoire.

Chapter 2

In the summer of 1949 the English-speaking Caerdydd branch of the Nationalist Party was able to have placed on the agenda of the Party Conference, to be held in Dyffryn Ardudwy in August that year, a motion that the aim of the Party be changed from 'Dominion Status within the British Commonwealth' to that of 'Independent Republic'. And thus, it was the hope of the young Republicans, Nationalist thinking could be moved into a new, a higher gear.

The Republican motion at Dyffryn Ardudwy suffered the expected defeat, the Conference vote being cast against it in a ratio of 9 to 1. But the debate had proceeded without undue accrimony on either side, and the Republican contingent, content that the issue had now at least been aired in full Conference, retired in good order to the Ardudwy seashore to make the most of that memorably pleasant summer weather.

But the last thing there could be any hope of a Conference decision extinguishing was the irrepressible spirit of Republican youth. A Conference of their own was convened in Castell Nedd (*Neath*) for the 24th and 25th of the following month, September 1949. Trefor Morgan was appointed to the Conference Chair. A decision was made to establish The Welsh Republican Movement — Mudiad Gweriniaethol Cymru, which was to be independent of any other political organization. Its governing authority was to be vested in a Council composed of members who would be equal in status and who would be appointed by a Congress of members of the Movement. The Movement's policy was to be defined in the Statement of Policy already prepared in draft form and to be published forthwith.

In the Conference Chairman's words could be summed up the whole enthusiastic tenor of that occasion: he took pride, he said, in the fact that at last there was in Wales a Movement encompassing the true meaning and dignity of her nationality.

> "The aim of establishing a free Welsh Republic is a truly worthy one for this Movement we have brought into existence to secure our nation's freedom. We have to create at once a new tradition of standing and fighting for the life and vital interests of our country.

The Republican Movement must step without delay into the political arena and contest the next Parliamentary Election in a way that will compel England to take notice that she must respect the full and just rights of the Welsh people."

The Movement adopted as its political emblem a tricolour flag of red, white and green.

With the formal establishment of their Movement behind them the activists intensified their efforts to make impact upon political opponents and those they accused of having betrayed their national inheritance. This was the period of complete Labour Party domination in the Westminster parliament of the immediate post-war years. And a time of complete disillusionment for many who might once have looked towards the Labour Party in the hope that the memory of its early ideal of self-government for the Celtic nations of Britain would not be forgotten. But forgotten it seemed to be — or if not forgotten, then cynically disowned.

James Griffiths, Minister of Pensions in that Labour government, was the instrument that Clement Attlee as Prime Minister, Herbert Morrison as Home Secretary, and Emmanuel Shinwell as War Minister and other fellow members in English government, had so conveniently at hand to convey that cynical repudiation to the people of Wales. In consequence, it was the misfortune of James Griffiths, seemingly quite ready to fulfil that rôle, that he had to bear much of the brunt of the Republicans' anger.

There was a fierce clash with him later that Autumn at a meeting in Garnant in the east of old Sir Gâr (*Carmarthenshire*). Half a dozen or so Republicans faced him at close quarters from the front two rows in the village hall. First, one of them rose to question and then accuse, before sitting again; then rising again and again to pursue the contention. He remembers a James Griffiths apologist, 'Llygad Llwchwr', columnist of the London daily, *The News Chronicle*, who was sitting behind him, begging him, hand on shoulder, to 'give the Minister a fair hearing, old man . . . ' But Griffiths was too much the target of righteous anger that night. That Republican remembers, half in affection, the two or three stocky Garnant miners who threw him out of the hall. And next he remembers a smart brown hat come skimming gracefully through the air in the light from the open door, followed by its owner, Trefor Morgan, unceremoniously propelled in its wake. And after a few minutes again came Haydn Jones, and then in their turn, others of the Republicans.

With the formal declaration of its existence there came many applications to join the Movement. Membership application forms stipulated a monthly payment to the Movement of two shillings per month, and membership cards for the first year were accordingly issued with provision for the recording of monthly payments from October onwards. This system of stepped payment was helpful to many members and drew an encouraging influx of membership from the student population in particular. Numbered amongst those early members are the names of people, past and present, who have achieved distinction in varying degrees in the life of Wales, or elsewhere in the world. At least three of them, members of the Movement's Governing Council, Ifor Wilks, Tom Williams and Graham Hughes attained professorships in their particular academic disciplines.

At about this time Gwilym Prys Davies became the owner of a quite large and elegant Riley car, which was kept, as far as recollection goes, at the home of his future wife, Llinos, in Abercynon. With Gwilym, Huw Davies, Gwyndaf Beriah Evans (then working with the South Wales Electricity Board as an overhead linesman, who was beginning to play an important practical part in Movement activities) and Cliff Bere, the only member of the crew with a driving licence, on board, the car was used now and again on political forays in the Valleys. A joking but not quite accurate remark by Huw Davies that Bere had been a tank driver in the North African desert probably hastened the resolve of the car's owner to pass his driving test.

With the assistance of new members the sale of Welsh Republican literature on the streets and at the door began to attract attention and, of course, its due share of argument concerning the Republican standpoint. But the members of the now officially constituted governing Council of the Movement had more immediate issues to concern them. In a letter dated 14th October 1949 to Huw Davies, Trefor Morgan, writing from Aberaman in the Cynon Valley, stressed the need to call a meeting of the Council of the Movement to discuss the impending general election. "Things seem to be livening up in Ogwr," he says, "and it would seem more than ever necessary to preserve the honour of Wales by continuing the fight there" (Trefor had contested the Ogwr (*Ogmore Vale*) parliamentary seat in 1946 as a Welsh Nationalist and achieved a very creditable vote of 5,685).

His letter goes on to suggest that Huw Davies and 'others of us' should go with him to Merthyr Tydfil where Trefor had recently been, in order to, in his own words, "try to unearth any support there might be there for the WRM". The letter continues: "By incredible good fortune I hit on a Mr Davies there who is very, very influential in local politics. In point of fact, he was one of the eight people who first nominated Keir Hardie for Merthyr. I discussed the purpose of my visit with him, and the upshot of it was that he was greatly in favour of fighting the seat and, by way of a start to the proposed venture, he volunteered an initial donation of ten guineas. In order to get a judgment upon the prospect at Merthyr other than my own, perhaps you would like to come as suggested in order to see for yourself."

There is no evidence amongst the WRM papers, nor memory, that Trefor's suggestion was taken up.

However, the talk of parliamentary elections that was in the air turned the attention of the more activist of the Republicans towards the very focal point of such elections, and so four or five members of the Movement contrived to obtain via their constituency MPs invitations to the visitors' gallery of the Westminster House of Commons for the occasion of the 'Welsh Debate' there on the 24th November 1949.

"Today's Welsh Debate in the House of Commons opened in a sensational manner," said a press report of the proceedings. "Within a few minutes of Mr James Griffiths, Minister of National Insurance, taking his place at the dispatch box to deliver the opening speech there was an uproar in the Private Members' Gallery. The House was startled when a loud shout of 'Quisling' was directed at Mr Griffiths, who had scarcely completed his opening sentence. With one exception all eyes turned to the gallery where a woman stood holding a red, green and white flag. The exception was Mr Griffiths who, ignoring the disturbance, attempted to make himself heard above the din. In less than a minute the demonstrator, Mrs Joyce Ann Williams, Chaddesley Terrace, Swansea, was seized by attendants and special police officers and forcibly ejected. But not before she had shouted again: 'You are a Quisling, Jim Griffiths. Go back to Wales. We want a Welsh Republic.'

"Scarcely had the young woman been removed from the gallery", goes on the report, "than another interruption took place. This time it was a young man who stood up in the same gallery. He took up where his colleague had left off. Again the charge of 'Quisling' was hurled at Mr Griffiths, and before other attendants could reach him and forcibly silence him he had shouted, 'Away with you, Jim Griffiths. Get back to Wales. We want a Welsh Socialist Republic'. He then showered members below with leaflets. Some fell over the Speaker's chair, but most of them fell amongst Conservative MPs. The man's name was given as Haydn Jones, a 27 year-old man from Ynysmeudwy, Pontardawe."

It is hard to repress a smile on reading that the one exception whose eyes were not turned to the gallery was James Griffiths himself. It was as if by now he was becoming inured to the expectation of these sudden, determined Republican harassments.

The report proceeds: "Supervision by police and attendants on public visitors to the House was increased after the initial disturbance, but yet another took place early in the evening. It happened when Mr John Evans (Ogmore) was addressing the House. From the side gallery a young man who had just been admitted showered another bundle of leaflets onto the Members' benches. He shouted, 'Get back to Wales', and his other remarks were muffled by attendants who forcibly ejected him. He joined his friends of the Welsh Republican Movement in the custody of the police. His name was given as Clifford Beri (sic), Wyndham Road, Cardiff." He had waited to go in after confirming from the Stop Press in the evening papers that the initial demonstration had been staged.

"In accordance with the rules of the House each will be blacklisted and forbidden to enter the precincts of Westminster Palace" (which does not reflect well on the security arrangements of that palace, as Bere, with others, attended there again in the early 1980s before the Minister at the Home Office (Elton) to present and argue a petition and appeal against the unjust refusal of parole to John B. Jenkins then being held in Dartmoor prison).

The leaflets thrown down on the floor of the House were the Welsh Republican Movement's newly published 12-point Manifesto, together with a single sheet leaflet printed in bold type by the Republicans themselves on their own small printing machine.

Another report of the occasion from the *News Chronicle* of 25/11/49 asks: "Who were the interrupters? Most of us thought they belong to the Nationalist Party's commando force, but Professor W.J. Gruffydd (member for the University of Wales) during his speech declared them to be members of the Welsh Republican Party. 'The Nationalist Party', he said, 'has already got old-fashioned'. The woman is from the Rhondda." (Joyce Williams is the daughter of the late Jacob Herbert, Dentist, and his wife Margaret of 20 High Street, Glynrhedyn (*Ferndale*).

The three prisoners were released around midnight in time to catch the 1 a.m. train back to Cymru.

Chapter 3

Now, the Movement was beginning to make its mark — in more than one field. For instance, in December 1949 there is an interesting comment in *The Courier*, the English language magazine of Aberystwyth University College students. After stating that the Movement had already set up a boundary commission to win back for Wales "its former territory before its confiscation by England," it goes on to say: "May we wish for this unique political prodigy in our midst every success in its enterprising venture, and let us remember that wherever it may go it will always be one of our very own babies."

Perhaps this rather overstated a progenitorial claim; but nevertheless it may not have been made without a certain degree of justification, for, in addition to producing important members of the Movement, it was the Nationalist students of Aberystwyth who helped to reduce to debacle what was no other than a recruiting mission made to Aberystwyth in 1947 by Emmanuel Shinwell, War Minister in London government.

The Movement had made application to Maesteg Urban District Council for permission to hold public meetings in the market yard in the vicinity of the Town Hall on occasional Saturday afternoons. This was granted in a letter dated 23rd November 1949 from the Clerk to the Council, subject to payment of a small fee, and very soon after a very well attended Republican meeting was held there. However, in the very near future Maesteg was to be the venue of another, and much more tumultuous gathering, and this time in the Town Hall itself.

The meeting in the spacious and quite impressive Town Hall building on 13th December 1949 was held to introduce to the people of Maesteg and district the new Labour candidate for the Ogwr (*Ogmore*) Division in the forthcoming general election, a Mr Walter Padley from the South of England. An indication of the potential for the dissension and eventual disturbance which characterized the meeting is conveyed in an excerpt from a letter written by Harri Webb in 1977 in reply to a request from someone asking for his recollections of the 1950 election in Ogwr.

"The situation as I recall it," wrote Harri Webb, "was that Labour was still in power with its massive post-war 1945 mandate, and, in the

South of Wales, the total loyalty of the people to an extent which it is now difficult to appreciate. Their MP for Ogmore (I'm afraid I forget his name) had been appointed High Commissioner for Australia and there had been a by-election. The local establishment replaced him by an ancient and inarticulate hack called John Evans, the sort of insult they so often dished out to their faithful constituencies, and in the subsequent by-election they were opposed by Trefor Morgan, who notched up a surprising vote, out of all proportion to anything Plaid Cymru had ever scored till then, something like 6,000 votes, I believe, a severe shock to Labour. Trefor (I'm not even sure whether he stood as official Plaid Cymru at all; he was a great individualist) fought a colourful campaign, of which some good stories are still told. So when the 1950 general election loomed, the Labour Party played safe and decided to get rid of the embarrassing John Evans. A native of the place was Rhys Davies, Labour MP for somewhere in the North of England and an official of the Union of Shop, Distributive and Allied Workers, and he was the agency by which Padley, also of USDAW, was 'parachuted' (as the French say) into Ogwr. John Evans's cronies were most put out and the Labour Party locally was bedevilled with feuds."

So the scene was set for another, by now almost inevitably hectic happening. *The Glamorgan Gazette* of 16th December 1949 made great play of the occasion, devoting the greater part of its front page spread to it, and in so doing undoubtedly deriving some degree of *Schadenfreud* — like satisfaction itself from so newsworthy an event involving no little degree of embarrassment to the party of government. "The prospective Labour candidate for the Ogmore Division, Mr Walter Padley," it said, "was continually heckled when he spoke at the Town Hall, Maesteg, on Monday. The interruptions were caused by a young married woman and four members of the Welsh Republican Movement. As soon as Mr Padley prepared himself to speak, the woman heckler stood up and shouted amid protests: 'Get back to England. We are a Welsh Republican Movement. You have no right to speak in Wales . . . Get back to England!'

"There were more interruptions and Councillor Stanley Lewis (Chairman of the meeting) declared: 'This is a definite attempt to break up this meeting. I am not going to allow these interruptions, but we would welcome them to ask questions afterwards'. When Mr Padley again tried to continue, a man in the body of the audience shouted: 'We want a Welshman', and kept shouting as he was escorted from the meeting. At this stage in the meeting the police were sent for, and four police officers who attended remained in the hall until the end of the meeting."

The Western Mail (14/12/49) reported: "Members of the Welsh Republican Party continually heckled Mr Walter Padley, president of the Allied and Distributive Workers' Union, prospective socialist candidate for Ogmore, during his campaign speech at Maesteg Town-hall last night, and eventually the police were called.

"Mr Padley faced interruptions from a young married woman and three young men. Three times he was shouted down amid protests from supporters, and the Chairman, Mr Stanley Lewis, had to make repeated appeals for order. Finally he asked the stewards to fetch the police.

"Five policemen arrived, and an officer escorted one young Welshman from the hall. Later, another man was removed by four civilians after he had shouted: 'We are governed by English imperialists. The government has done nothing for Wales.' "

★ ★ ★

There is a sad, even bitter irony in the fact that it was against the representatives of a Labour government that the Welsh Republican Movement in these first years of its existence should find itself having to flex its youthful political muscle. Socialism in its most civilized, humane conception was the Movement's creed. Its enemy was toryism in all its manifestations. And the toryism suffusing English politics was also the enemy of the early leaders of the Labour party; they were alive to the political oppression that was inherent in London rule over Wales and Scotland and Ireland. Self-government for England's three sister nations of the British Isles was accordingly an integral part of their socialist, democratic policy.

But, in paraphrase of the words of *The Welsh Republic*, as it had become a force in English political life the English Labour Party had begun to temper and sometimes abandon entirely its initial idealism. Self-government for Wales and Scotland had been abandoned. And in doing so the English Labour Party had betrayed the fundamental principle of democracy — the right of nations to govern themselves.

It was not a small thing to abandon the principle of freedom for nations — to deny the very premise of democracy. But that was the unanswerable indictment which had to stand against the English Labour Party of that day. It was the measure of its compromise with the anti-democracy of toryism.

A quote from the Welsh Gossip column of political observer Llygad Llwchwr in the London *News Chronicle* in 1954 makes a relevant comment on this sad situation: "Labour politicians were almost unanimously in favour of self-government (for the Celtic nations) before the 1945 General Election. A crack of Mr Herbert Morrison's whip drove most of them up another lane to the barren moorland of English political expedience."

Chapter 4

On the 28th December 1949 on the striking red and green headed notepaper of the Welsh Republican Movement Tom Williams wrote from 1, Chaddesley Terrace, Abertawe to Harri Webb:

"Annwyl Harri Webb,

I take the liberty of introducing myself. Ithel Davies tells me that you are interested in helping us to play hell with Padley in Ogmore. I should like to get in touch with you as I understand you can help us with press publicity. You probably know by now that Ithel will be our candidate at Ogmore (If you do not, keep this to yourself). It will be let out to the press on Wednesday, 4th January next. Could you help us with this?

I understand that you now live in Cardiff — you may like to get into touch with our Secretary there, Huw Dafis, 8, Lôn-y-Rhyd, Cardiff.

Cofion fil,
Tom Williams

P.S. I very much enjoyed your 'Walter, Walter, lead me by the halter . . . ' More of that is needed. I shall be at 20, High Street, Ferndale for the next week or so.

T.W."

Harri Webb had been collaborating with Keidrych Rhys in Caerfyrddin in the publication of the literary magazine *Wales*, but had recently moved to Caerdydd and had taken up employment in a bookshop in the Queen Street Station approach. Before that he had done a very brief stint as a uniformed commissionaire at a cinema in the city. Although as yet unknown to the main body of the Republicans, he had obviously already felt prompted to take up a wit-barbed pen to enter the fray - at Ogwr in particular. A few months earlier he had come across a copy of *The Welsh Republic* in a small newsagent's shop, Thomas' in Maes Nott, Caerfyrddin.

The record shows that Harri Webb was formally enrolled as a member of the Welsh Republican Movement on the 16th January 1950.

A few days earlier, as reported in *Y Faner ac Amserau Cymru* of 11/1/1950,

James Griffiths had addressed a meeting in Porth Tywyn (*Burry Port*), where once again he took the opportunity to level his by now characteristically wild charge of Nazism against the Republicans. Referring to a statement in a Welsh newspaper in the previous October where a member of WRM had been said to have expressed the need to choose an able Cymro from amongst the people as leader, Griffiths had chosen to interpret this to his audience that night as an 'expression of Nazi ideology and the führer principle'.

It was surely a sign that he was, temporarily at least, being driven not a little off balance, or even a degree hysterical, by the attention he had been receiving at the hands of the Republicans. "I believe," he said at the meeting, "that these Republicans are so fond of me that they follow me everywhere, even to the House of Commons to interfere with my speeches." The force of Republican indignation was obviously leaving its mark on James Griffiths, and its indelible impression is quite possibly reflected in the fact that when the office of Secretary of State for Wales was first created in 1964 and offered to him, he accepted the appointment only on his stipulation that it would be invested with a worthwhile and practical degree of authority concerning the very few matters of administration devolved to it at the outset.

★ ★ ★

In a meeting on 14/15th January 1950 at Abertawe the Council of the Welsh Republican Movement decided to formally nominate Ithel Davies as its candidate to contest the Ogwr constituency at the forthcoming general election. That decision was a great — and possibly undeserved — disappointment for Trefor Morgan, who had gained 5,685 votes in the 1946 by-election at Ogwr. He had supporters for his candidature in the meeting. He and they pressed the case for also fighting the Merthyr seat, where Trefor had made an exploratory investigation into the situation there and had received some promise of support. But this proposal, like John Legonna's suggestion of contesting the Ceredigion seat, where he had farming interests at Ffynnon Gloch, Llanarth, and elsewhere in the county, was outvoted for the simple reason that the financial resources of the Movement would be more than fully committed at Ogwr alone.

Cliff Bere was appointed to be election agent to the candidate at a salary to help him maintain himself, his wife and newly born son over the period of the election.

At the same meeting it was decided to proceed at once with the issue of a periodical news-sheet in the form of a cyclostyled Republican Bulletin. The first of these, dated January 1950, was produced within the next few days. It announced the candidature of Ithel Davies, saying: "Our candidate goes into the struggle, pledged never to take an oath of allegiance to the king of England,

and bound by the implacable determination of all Welsh Republicans that the sway of England over Wales shall be destroyed." An editorial note says: "The Council hope that from this modest start will grow the first periodical of the Movement."

Under the heading 'Achievements of 1949' it lists the 'Welsh Day' at Westminster, paying tribute to the three members who took part in its disruption.

Then, on Shinwell, Griffiths and Padley — "These three unfortunate worthies have felt an inkling of the wrath of a long-suppressed Wales . . . The rousing welcome given to English War Minister Shinwell on his abortive recruiting visit to Aberystwyth was led and inspired by Welsh Republicans. England's much-vaunted recruiting machine was made the laughing stock of its own House of Commons. Dr James Griffiths MP, London representative in Llanelli, ran into a Republican storm at Garnant on his own 'tump' when he sought to decry the national aims of his own people. English trade union boss, Walter Padley, who presumes to stand as parliamentary candidate in Ogmore, was shouted down in his first election meeting at Maesteg."

The hand of Huw Davies is seen at the bottom of page 3 of the Bulletin: *"Gair i'n darllenwyr Cymraeg: Yn yr iaith fain yr ysgrifennir y rhan fwyaf o'r Bwletin hwn. Yn Saesneg hefyd y cynhelir y rhan fwyaf o weithgarwch y Mudiad. Nid yw hyn yn golygu diystyrwch o werth ein hiaith fawreddog. Ond i holl genedl y Cymry y mae ein neges ni."*

On page 4 is listed the history of literature sales over the past six months, with mention of well over twenty towns visited.

Under the heading 'Celtic Co-operation', there is: "The possibilities of a live inter-Celtic Front are boundless. Contacts with Brittany and Ireland are being strengthened. One of our members has addressed a Scots Republican Socialist meeting near Glasgow. *The Celtic Time* is sold by some of our members on the streets to help the growth of the Celtic idea in Wales. With the help of our Celtic friends the disintegration of England's 'Britain' can be brought rapidly nearer."

★ ★ ★

Towards the end of January Cliff Bere, as candidate's agent, and Huw Davies, who had taken a period of leave for the period of the election from his employment as export executive with Cory Bros., Caerdydd, moved into lodgings at 39, Coity Road, Pen-y-bont ar Ogwr (*Bridgend*). There are memories of the intensely cold weather as in the narrow confines of their room they set about preparing for the work ahead. But within a few days they had been able to rent an empty shop in Park Street from Mr Trevor David, a well-known personality in the town, and a man with his own very distinctive brand of political ideas.

Almost as soon as the election HQ had been established there were visits from the press, for the Republican idea was considered eminently newsworthy and several reports of interviews and articles appeared, some useful and informative, others more imaginative than factual.

The task the Republicans faced with their limited resources, human and financial, was formidable. The Ogwr electoral division extended over a width of twenty miles and covered a hundred square miles of coastal plain and mining valleys. Its electorate numbered 56,000, widespread between small towns and villages near the coast, and close-knit and congested in the several valleys leading northwards up to the hills bordering the Rhondda.

The candidates in opposition to Ithel Davies were Walter Padley, Labour, Mavis Llewellyn, Communist, and Raymond Gower, Tory.

60,000 Republican election addresses were printed and the practical work involved in despatching these taxed resources to the utmost. The Republican election posters in bold black block, we thought well-entitled to claim, made a better show than those of the other parties.

Our campaign was conducted with the help of probably no more than a score of supporters there together at any one time, and with most of these commuting from outside the constituency. The few local helpers included the redoubtable Ted Merriman from Nant-y-moel, a prominent and very active figure in the mining community. When things were going well we had the use of three cars at our disposal, one of them equipped with a loudspeaker.

Ithel Davies was present in Ogwr throughout almost the whole of the three weeks leading up to polling day on 23rd February. He spoke eloquently and tirelessly at the many meetings held at various places throughout the constituency. A memory remains of a spirited supporting speech at one of the meeting by Mrs Hannah Reynolds Davies, native of Pontycymer in the Garw Valley, the attractive, talented mother of Huw Davies.

★ ★ ★

At the beginning of February the Bangor and District Group of WRM issued 'Llais y Gogledd' — 'Voice of the North', a cyclostyled four page news-sheet on the pattern of the already published WRM 'Bulletin'. It was well and effectively written (mainly in English) with reference to matters of particular interest in the North. One, under the heading — 'Conway Castle — a Note on National Unity' ran as follows:

> "The Ministry of Works have already attempted to take over the guardianship of Conway Castle from the Borough. Determined to retain their local control, the Conway Council have been stirred from

their ancient calm. One Alderman of that proud Borough, outraged by the high-handed treatment of the deputation sent from Conway to the Ministry of Works, declared: 'Let us have a government for Wales and let Wales decide her own destiny'.

"It is one of the tragedies of Welsh life today", the piece goes on, "that her people only rise above age-old servility to England when their own individual interests are threatened. One day it is Conway Castle and the Ministry of Works; the next it is the Trawsfynydd farmers and the War Office; the next, Penmachno farmers and the Forestry Commission; the next, derelict tenements and the absentee landlord; the next, the closure of a pit and the Coal Board. And the next — who knows?

"The glaring fact in all these cases is that ultimately it is always the will of the attacker which prevails, and always the Welsh people who suffers. And so it will always be, until the men and women of Wales realize that their own interests are bound up with the Welsh, and NOT the English nation, and until they declare with the Conway Alderman, 'Let Wales decide her own destiny'. Until then, the traditional Welsh battle for democracy and social justice can never succeed!"

There follows a telling piece about the injustice of the BBC's refusal to grant broadcasting time to the candidates of the Welsh Nationalist Party in the forthcoming election, although in fielding seven candidates the Nationalists were contesting 20% of the seats in Wales. "Yet time is denied them!" it protests. "Of this grave injustice, we can only agree with a Welsh Party spokesman that 'It is the latest of the 1000 and one reasons for a Parliament for Wales.' "

There are articles on unemployment, on the injustice of military conscription, and, of course, one at length on the impending election, ending with the words: "Free from England, Wales will prevail over the hated forces of reaction and evil which have hitherto been dominant within her borders. In the Republic, old antipathies between Liberal, Labour and Communist will fall away, meaningless, and the unstultified will of the people, y werin bobl, will raise Wales to the highest dignity which a peace-loving and self-governing nation can attain."

The activities of the Bangor Group were not confined to political matters. The poet R.S. Thomas accepted an invitation to address them, and this he did on the subject of literature in Wales written in English.

The Republican platform in the election was based on the twelve points of the Welsh Republican Manifesto, the English version of which reads as follows:

> 1. That Wales must be a sovereign democratic Republic subject only to such authority as it may accept or subscribe to as a member of the community of free nations.
> 2. That the king of England whether in person as liege lord or through any constitutional agency as monarch shall have no jurisdiction in or dominion over Wales or any person in Wales.
> 3. That no Welshman or Welsh woman shall owe allegiance to or be the subject of any liege lord or any other person.
> 4. That there shall be in Wales no hereditary or other titles or any other form of political or social or economic prerogatives or distinctions nor any privileges which are not shared or capable of being shared by all.
> 5. The people of Wales shall be a free people in a free country and not subject to any servitudes whether political, social or economic and shall enjoy in their society a status of unqualified equality. All class distinctions whether based on claims of birth or property shall be abolished.
> 6. The Republic of Wales shall be founded upon the unreserved recognition of the dignity and worth of the human personality and shall guarantee to the people of Wales without distinction the unrestricted rights of the moral person in order to secure and promote the fullest development of the individual person and of the national life.
> 7. It shall be the aim of the Republic of Wales to bring to consummation the idea of the democratic society in all fields of human activity and interest and establish the principle of co-operation as the democratic basis of our economy in the form of co-operative organisations or guilds in which the work, the responsibilities and the fruits shall be shared by all who work.
> 8. To the same end ownership shall be by and for use only. All the archaic forms of land tenure shall be abolished and land, houses and all other properties shall vest in those who for living purposes or for work use them either individually or in co-operation as co-owners.
> 9. The Welsh language as the native language of the Welsh people shall be the first and official language of the Republic of Wales but in the circumstances which have resulted in Wales through English rule the English language shall be used as a second language and as such shall be officially recognised.
> 10. It shall be a primary aim of the Republic of Wales to increase the

acreage of Welsh land under food production and to establish a balanced Welsh economy by means of a vigorous policy of land settlement and development of rural trades and industries.

11. The Republic of Wales shall live in close association with all the other Celtic peoples and shall endeavour in every way to co-operate fully with all other nations and particularly with its near neighbours in the Republic of Ireland, Scotland and England.

12. The Republic of Wales must have and take its place and play its part in the international community of nations.

The Welsh Republican Manifesto was published separately in Welsh and English versions. Its twelve aims were also included in the second published edition of Cliff Bere's *The Welsh Republic*.

Republican meetings throughout the election campaign had in general been sparsely attended. But the final meeting in the big hall in Gilfach Goch on the evening before polling day gave good promise of making up for that to some extent. It turned out to be a densely packed gathering of a thousand or more people who had come to listen to the winding up addresses of the four candidates, who would each have an allotted time to put his or her party's case. Walter Padley spoke first and received the applause of the greater part of the audience. Raymond Gower's speech had a decidedly quieter reception. Mavis Llewellyn drew much warmer applause. As scheduled, Ithel had to speak last; but already, after something approaching two hours of patient listening, many of the audience were beginning to leave. In spite of this, our candidate made the mistake of sticking to his carefully prepared, measured brief. By the time he had finished the hall was well more than half empty. It was an opportunity lost — and it was in a subdued mood that we travelled back in the car to Pen-y-bont that night, with Ithel like the others of us well conscious of that fact.

★ ★ ★

In a letter published in *The Glamorgan Advertiser* on 17/3/50 Ithel Davies wrote — "to thank those gallant 613 people who voted for me in the General Election, for their confidence and support . . . They did what the nationals of every nation do with intense emotional pride . . . We are a small Movement with a very great purpose. That purpose we will pursue to its triumphant conclusion."

An issue of the WRM 'Bulletin' made reference for comparison, to the 609 votes for Lewis Valentine in Caernarfon in 1930 in the Welsh Nationalist Party's first parliamentary contest, and the 598 votes gained by John Burns in 1885 as the first candidate of the Labour Party in these islands. "This election is over", the 'Bulletin' said. "Some patriots may be disheartened with the result. Not so the Republicans!" — as events of the following years were to bear out.

There is a memorable quote at that time from Harri Webb for whom the election had come as a baptism in Republican activities — "Ithel Davies' score of 613 is graven not on its tombstone, but on its foundation stone" — a prophecy which all sincere patriots carry in their hearts and minds to this day.

In the Welsh language paper *Y Cymro* of 24th March 1950 reference was made to the ineffectual attempt by Plaid Cymru to make a case for denying to the Republicans the use in their Welsh language literature of the hallowed word 'Gweriniaeth' as the meaning of 'Republic'.

"Some prominent members of Plaid Cymru maintain", reports the paper, "that Ithel Davies and his followers have no right to the name 'Gweriniaeth'; they insist on calling them 'Ripyblicanod' ". One of Plaid Cymru's prominent and very respected members is quoted as saying: "Gan fy mod i'n credu mai ym Mhlaid Cymru y mae'r mynegiant cyflawn i radicaliaeth y werin Gymreig a bod gwerthoedd hanfodol gweriniaeth yn ei hathroniaeth hi, ni allaf gydsynio â hawl mudiad y Ripyblicanwyr mai hwy biau'r gair ardderchog 'gweriniaeth'."

This was a rather sad effort by that particular Plaid Cymru spokesman to distort language for a petty political end. However, it must be said, it was quite uncharacteristic of him.

Two years later it was he who baptized the second son of Cliff and Eluned Bere, Gareth, in Bargoed.

But the issue concerning the use of 'Gweriniaeth', if issue it ever became, was at an end almost before it began, for it was soon, if not already, in current usage with its republican meaning by everyone writing of politics in Welsh, including Mr Saunders Lewis.

There is a sad footnote to the chapter of events covering the Republican intervention in the Ogwr election of 1950: Trefor Morgan in his disappointment felt unable to join us in the work of the campaign in Ogwr and we in our turn felt deeply the loss of so experienced and invaluable a helper.

But Trefor did not intend to be denied his ambition to stand in that election of 1950. With the help of the support, political and financial, which he had previously suggested to his Republican colleagues was to be found in Merthyr, he stood there as an Independent Welsh Nationalist. He obtained 1,571 votes, as against 29,210 for S.O. Davies (Labour) and 6,294 for L.E. Haddrill (Conservative). It is interesting to conjecture what the vote for the Welsh Republican candidate in Ogwr might have been if he had had the undoubted political flair of Trefor to call on to help him in his campaign. Or even perhaps if Trefor himself had been chosen to be the Republican candidate there.

But it was as if these disappointments suffered had emancipated Trefor, to some degree at least, from the siren call of political activity, and so allow him to concentrate his flair and acumen in business and commercial matters towards the founding of the successful 'Undeb' Insurance Company, and which in due course enabled him and his wife Gwyneth to take an important initiative towards widening the scope of Welsh language education.

Chapter 5

In April following the Cwm Ogwr election a party from the Welsh Republican Movement crossed the water to Dulyn (*Dublin*) where Ithel Davies and Tom Williams addressed a Conference of the Irish Anti-Partition Alliance. Whilst there, Ithel Davies had a lengthy talk with Seán MacBride, Ireland's Minister for External Affairs (who later became an influential figure on the world stage and was awarded the Nobel Prize for Peace in 1974), and this resulted in an invitation to the WRM to send representatives to the annual Conference of Clann na Poblachta, the new political party that MacBride was largely instrumental in founding in opposition to the two old-established parties there. The fact that this invitation was never formally taken up, despite the enthusiasm it initially generated, is probably, but not soley perhaps, due to unfortunate events in the Spring of the following year, the recording of which will be left to take its place in the chronological order of this story.

It was about this time too, that Gwilym Prys Davies and Cliff Bere made a visit together to Scotland to try to further contact with allies there in the cause of Celtic freedom.

But it was on home territory in Wales that the pace of events was soon to accelerate and stir into symbolic action. On a Saturday afternoon, the 6th of May 1950, a group of Republicans symbolically burnt the Union Jack flag at a meeting outside the Market Place in Castell Nedd (*Neath*). "The flag of every nation is a sacred symbol of its pride of nationality", said one of the speakers. "The flag of England is the plain Cross of Saint George, and as such is respected by us. But that which we as Welsh Republicans are going to set fire to today, a contrived combination of the national flags of Ireland, Scotland and England — on which, please note, it has not been thought worthwhile to represent Wales — is not the proud flag of any nation, but rather a banner of device symbolizing the conquest and/or subsequent annexation and domination over the Celtic nations of Britain by an imperialist England. As such, we burn it with impunity."

As a result a considerable crowd of onlookers had assembled, from amongst whom, as a column in the Welsh press reported, a man had raised his voice above the mixture of approbation and other lively comment that followed as the burning remnants fell to the road. "Can the speakers make it clear that they are not communists?" he asked. Through his speaking horn the Chairman of the meeting, Huw Davies, told him: "Of that I can assure you. It is Welsh Republicans declaring the right of the people of Wales to sovereignty and political authority for themselves who are proud to stand here before you today."

This event of the public burning by the Welsh Republicans in Castell Nedd of the symbol of England's imperialism was the first of many such at Republican meetings on the streets of the towns and villages of Wales during the next year or two.

One of the most memorable of these meetings staged around the burning of the hated emblem was the one in Aberafan (*Port Talbot*) following the event in Castell Nedd two weeks earlier. It was held alongside the A48 road in the middle of the town at the height of the busy Saturday afternoon rush of people and traffic. The M4 motorway was still a project of the future, and the A48, in those days the main road link between Caerdydd and Abertawe and further west, passed through the centre of the town.

Some hundreds of people quickly gathered. The crowd surging around the speakers seemed to be made up in fairly equal proportions between those who were shouting or showing approval, and those who were not. The Republicans were able to face them confidently, well aware that the Republican name already carried its aura and suggestion of readiness to face up to challenge. All motor traffic along the road had been forced to a halt. Policemen were seen hovering on the outskirts of the crowd, seemingly helpless to make any effective move towards dispersing it.

"Some hundreds of people had gathered by now and were imperilling traffic on the main road between Swansea and Cardiff", said a press report at the time. "A number of policemen came to clear the crowd away, but without success. The sergeant appealed to the speakers to move back in order to help to clear the road." The Republicans who spoke at that meeting were Huw Davies, Cliff Bere, and Tom and Joyce Williams.

That emblem was burnt again at a successful Republican meeting on the east promenade of Porthcawl on the following 10th of June.

★ ★ ★

As already mentioned, the Republicans were able to print on their small Adana press (a far cry from the ease and efficiency of present-day desk top printing) their own very presentable leaflets in prominent block type. These were produced in their thousands by Gwyndaf Beriah Evans, then of Clodien Avenue, Caerdydd, who had been a core member of the Movement from almost the day of its founding.

A typical product of the little press, when the threat of conscription and re-call to armed forces hung over the youth of Wales, exhorted as follows in its bold print:-

IF WAR COMES
THE WELSH REPUBLICANS CALL ON YOU TO SERVE WALES
Citizens of Wales -- give NO ALLEGIANCE to
England's king and country
WELSHMEN - BOYCOTT ENGLAND'S ARMED FORCES
Join the Welsh Republican Campaign
NO MORE BLOOD FOR ENGLAND
WE SERVE NEITHER KING NOR KREMLIN
WALES FIRST
AND WALES A REPUBLIC

Leaflets such as these were distributed amongst the listeners at all Republican meetings. Although the uniformed police were often onlookers at these meetings, an incident of police interference at an earlier meeting in Porthcawl in the previous year had been the only occasion hitherto when they had seen fit to stop a meeting proceeding to its end.

But on Saturday, 17th June, in the week following the Porthcawl meeting, on the occasion of a meeting held at the junction of Bute Street and Victoria Square in Aberdâr, there came a change in the tactics of the police. A group of four or five Republicans were present there on that fine sunny evening. A flag was burnt, and almost as if by magic the lower part of the Square became a great throng of 150 or more watching people, and as if by magic too, a row of five or six stalwart Glamorgan County police officers appeared close at hand to survey proceedings.

As a result of this meeting, the police brought two charges against the Republicans. The first was for 'unlawfully using insulting behaviour whereby a breach of the peace was likely to be occasioned contrary to The Public Order Act 1936, section 5.' The other was for the Common Law offence of 'obstructing the pathway by causing a crowd to assemble'. Summonses were issued against Tom and Joyce Williams and Cliff Bere on each of the two charges. The event received much publicity and the case was heard at Aberdâr on 26th July 1950 before a crusty old Stipendiary, Mr Joshua Davies, KC.

Despite peremptory rejections of well-thought-out submissions by them, the defendants were able to give a good account of themselves and pursued a keen cross-examination of all witnesses brought against them. However, the three were found guilty on the charge under The Public Order Act and were each fined £5 and 13sh. costs. The charge of causing an obstruction was dismissed. The magistrate announced an alternative of 14 days imprisonment on failure to pay the fine and costs within a fortnight.

The defendants intimated that they would appeal to the court of Quarter Sessions against their conviction.

"At this juncture", *The Aberdare Leader* newspaper reported, "Mrs Gwyneth Morgan, Aberaman (wife of Mr Trefor Morgan, Welsh Republican candidate at Merthyr in this year's General Election), jumped up at the back of the court and shouted 'Long live the Welsh Republicans'.

"The Stipendiary retaliated by ordering her to be removed from the courtroom immediately; but her lead was followed by other supporters of Welsh Republicanism who were present. There was a cry of 'Up the Welsh Republican Party', and a general hubbub followed as the courtroom emptied.

"In the corridor outside, Mrs Morgan was approached by Police-sergeant Albert Hailstone, who asked for her name and address.

"Outside, in Market Street, there were ten to a dozen police officers, who kept an eye on the defendants and their supporters as they moved away in the direction of Victoria Square and Canon Street. For some time after the court hearing had ended, a police car was on 'slow patrol' through the streets of the town."

A notice of appeal against conviction was duly entered, but, at some additional financial cost to the defendants, it was eventually decided not to proceed with it.

★ ★ ★

At the beginning of July 1950 the fourth issue of the Republican 'Bulletin' was published. Its six tightly packed cyclo-styled pages carried a wealth of comment and information. It began with a scathing comment on the 'milk-and-water' Home Rule Conference held at Llandrindod a few days earlier on the 1st of July, the organizers of which, commented 'The Bulletin', "chose not to extend an invitation to the Welsh Republican Movement — obviously, loyalty to the Union Jack was a minimum requirement for representation! However, despite their desire to ignore the only force that shows signs of effectively fighting for Welsh freedom, the Swansea branch of our Movement did send two representatives, who, needless to say, were safely tucked away in the rear."

'The Bulletin' comments concerning some of those there to represent different bodies and associations in Wales were often, to say the least, disparaging. But "S.O. Davies (despite his reference to the overworked 'Mother' of parliaments) spoke courageously, and his attendance, in face of the English Labour Party ban, will hardly increase his chance of promotion! And Welsh Party President Gwynfor Evans spoke well; most Republicans could agree with almost all he said. His point that no nation ever won freedom through a petition gave some reality to the proceedings. But his party fail to practise what they preach! His passive, pacifist leadership has led the Welsh Party into alliance with the moderates, who are the enemies of the Republic."

Ithel Davies, it reported, spoke well from the floor.

Under an item headed '*Flag on Fire!*' there is a report on the WRM open-air meeting campaign:

> "Our task is to build in Wales a tradition of political resistance strong enough to withstand and finally reject the destroying pressure of the English domination. Such a tradition is the only political institution that a subject nation can possess as the rallying point of its national pride and will to live. We have to draw out and forge the resistance that smoulders under the surface of Wales into the spearhead of the rebellion of our politically headless nation.
>
> "As the English imperial flag burns before the people on the squares and streets of Neath, Port Talbot, Tonypandy, Porth, Newport, Blackwood, Porthcawl, Aberdare, and the smaller valley towns, we can feel that those of the crowd who are bold enough to shout their encouragement speak not only for themselves but also for the majority of the onlookers. The silent acquiescence of the watching Welsh people is eloquent to us as only silence can be. As we proceed from meeting to meeting we know that a tradition is in process of formation — that a new spirit of resistance is beginning to kindle in the people of this subject nation.
>
> "And when we see an Englishman run to pick the ruins of his state flag from the gutter and shout, 'You'll never destroy the English empire!' we know, as though by divine foretelling, that there is, in his hands, the charred symbols of his arrogant nation's decline and fall. Let no one waste fears on the English! The sensitivity and civilization of the Welsh world has for far too long given way before the bluster of the English boor. But at last the Welsh are getting his measure. Today we are beginning to see the spirit of our people mustering on the squares of Wales against England in her rôle as destroyer of nations."

But perhaps the most important of 'The Bulletin's' several items was that which under the heading 'From strength to strength' announced the impending publication by the WRM of a printed newspaper: " . . . *The Welsh Republican — Y Gweriniaethwr*. Frequency of publication will be a matter under constant review; but the first number will be on sale by Eisteddfod week . . . The paper will retail at 2d. A subscription of 1s.6d. will cover the first six numbers, postage included . . . Huw Davies will edit the new *Welsh Republican*, assisted by a representative editorial board.

"So, to the young lions of the Republic we say: 'Out into the highways and byways of our land, selling! (The discount on every copy sold will swell your branch funds)'. To the constipated Canutes who cannot check the tide of our progress, we say, 'Buy and support, read and believe — *The Welsh Republican*'. Harri Webb (Managing Editor)"

The final item under the heading 'Council Meeting' discussed a report of the situation in the Tywi Valley area "where some 46 farms were threatened with extinction by the plans of the English Forestry Commission. The report stated that the farmers were all determined to resist the ill-conceived claims of the Commission, realizing that once again the whole pattern of Welsh life was in the balance due to the massive greed of the English power state. Attention was called to the fact that the English Minister of Agriculture had summarily refused to have the afforestation plans reconsidered. The WRM Council representative who visited the area under the shadow of the English master planners emphasized that already the inhabitants were talking freely of the revenge that would be taken against England if nothing were done to adopt a more reasoned policy. It would be a dread responsibility of the Minister concerned if anything untoward should occur in this rich and historic area of our country".

At the end of 'The Bulletin' Huw Davies reminded of 'Doethineb ein Hynafiaid — *Tri pheth anhawdd eu cael: nyth cog ym mhen derwen; cist cybydd heb glo; a thegwch gan Sais. (O Lyfr Trioedd Beirdd Ynys Prydain, casgliad 1650)*'.

Chapter 6

'UNION JACK MUST NOT BE BURNED' ran a big headline in *The South Wales Echo* of 9th August in Eisteddfod week 1950, reporting as follows:

"Though Wales was a nation with its own flag, individuality and culture, it must always remain loyal to the Union Jack said the Lord Mayor of Cardiff (Alderman George Williams) in his speech of welcome to overseas visitors at Caerphilly National Eisteddfod today.

"The Union Jack is the flag of the Commonwealth and Wales is one of the nations of the Commonwealth. That flag must never be burned, he said."

As our old friend 'Llygad Llwchwr' reported in his column in the London *News Chronicle* of 12th August a few days later, the Lord Mayor's speech created a 'sensation', for it was by no means unanimously well received by his Eisteddfod audience. "Because this column reported the reaction of the crowd to the well-meaning Lord Mayor of Cardiff", wrote the columnist, "the main leading article in the local Tory paper is quite angry with me this morning. It keeps a leading article in stock for Llygad Llwchwr. Today they have slightly diluted the Yorkshire-Welsh relish — I am now a mere trashy Nationalist. I like the previous description better: there is a good spicy taste about being called a Welsh Sinn Feiner."

But whether or not the two Republicans who climbed the tall tower of Caerffili Castle on the afternoon of Friday, 11th August in Eisteddfod week were acting in direct reaction to that mayoral injunction, it is difficult to remember. But climb it they did, via a ladder carelessly left pointing upwards to a gap high in a wall of the castle courtyard. From the top of the ladder a passageway in the wall led to steps giving access to their target — an enormous Union Jack measuring 16ft x 8ft, arrogantly flaunting its domination directly above the Eisteddfod field even on this unique once-yearly occasion of Eisteddfodic assembly and reunion for the Welsh people.

Quickly the flag was lowered, set afire, and raised again to the top of the mast, followed by a smart retreat (only momentarily delayed when one of the comrades took a wrong turn down the steps of an adjoining tower) and back to the top of the ladder.

Down in the courtyard visitors stood politely aside as two bodies descended at speed into their midst. But two police officers could already be seen running down the grass slope between the nearby police-station and the castle. Keeping to a leisurely pace amongst the sightseers because they were again in full view of the police, the two made their way round a sheltering corner, and then made off down a path out of the castle. But a burly sergeant and policeman, undeceived, came thundering after them. The sergeant, obviously exasperated at being caught out in his duty of surveillance on the castle and its flag, raised an arm to strike.

"You're a civil servant, aren't you? Then you'd better behave like one!" he was sharply told, and his arm was lowered.

The two Republicans were led back under arrest past very surprised visitors and to the police headquarters about a hundred yards away.

Within the next twenty minutes or so half the police heads of Glamorgan County seemed to have come together there to castigate and question the two men. The activities of the Welsh Republican Movement had obviously become a sore point with the police and those ultimately responsible for directing policing policy. The Republicans, Clifford Bere and Gwyndaf Evans, were released on bail and summoned to appear at Caerffili police court on 22nd August on a charge of 'causing malicious damage to a Union Jack flag contrary to section 51 of the Malicious Damages Act 1861'.

After a hearing that made interesting reading in a wide range of newspapers — "the accused, both married men with children, and who had pleaded not guilty, elected not to give evidence on oath and pursued a lengthy cross-examination of witnesses . . . They were fined £25 and £15 respectively and given seven days to pay the fines, but both stated they would be unable to do so."

Within the seven days they had entered notice of appeal to the court of Quarter Sessions, thereby deferring enforcement of payment of the fines, but withdrew their appeal three days before the next sitting of Quarter Sessions, and in consequence incurred a claim of £54:12:9 to cover alleged costs and expenses of the police in preparing to oppose the appeal.

They were summoned to court on 28th November 1950 to answer that claim made in the name of Police Superintendent William Folland, who was not present in court. The two Republicans requested his presence in order to cross-examine him on the details of the claim, "saying that they would ask for a case to be stated in the King's Bench Division of the High Court on a point of procedure if their request was not granted." The case was duly adjourned for a fortnight to allow the Superintendent to be present.

At the adjourned hearing on 12th December the Superintendent was closely questioned by the two, who insisted that there was a "fundamental difference between costs and expenses, and the only item on the bill we can agree with is one for 6s.8d."

After the justices had gone through the items the chairman of the Bench announced an amended amount of £29:19:9.

Nevertheless, Bere and Evans said they would give notice for a case to be stated in the High Court. As a result, they were eventually able to defer enforcement of payment of that amount until after a further police court hearing on 26th June 1951.

But one of the defendants in the Caerffili case was in court again very soon after the 12th December 1950 hearing. On the 20th December Tom and Joyce Williams and Clifford Bere had been summoned to Aberdâr Magistrate's court to face a claim by Police Superintendent J.J. Fitzpatrick for costs and expenses incurred in the aftermath of the police prosecution following the Victoria Square meeting in Aberdâr. The three defendants in that case had entered notice of appeal to Quarter Sessions against conviction, but, as already mentioned, had withdrawn the appeal before the hearing date. The police claim was for a sum of £53 for costs, etc. incurred by the police in preparing to oppose the appeal. The Republicans resisted the claim by alleging, according to one press report, "that Mr Roderick Bowen, M.P., had been the barrister chosen by the police to resist at Swansea Quarter Sessions on appeal against the conviction . . . because he was a Welsh patriot and was thus involved in 'a scheme to turn Welshman against Welshman'.

"When the Stipendiary Magistrate, Mr Joshua Davies, K.C., said the police would be awarded £46 costs Bere said, 'I refuse to accept your judgment. This is a travesty of justice'.

"When they continued to protest police officers accompanied them from the courtroom.

"Williams had interrupted the opening statement by Mr Graham Bird, for the police, to claim that a summons which had been delivered to him only on 16th December was wrongly drawn. It failed to mention under what Acts the claim was brought.

"The Magistrate: 'Where is your legal authority for that proposition?'

"Williams: 'I'll come to that later.'

" 'You must make your point now.'

" 'Very well, then. I withdraw that, but I would point out that this summons differs very much from the one issued in a similar case at Caerphilly.'

" 'Can you point to any law which says this summons must be similar to that at Caerphilly?' — 'All right, I withdraw that, but the summons as it stands implies that the costs have already been granted as a civil debt.'

"The Magistrate disallowed an application for an adjournment and Bere said, 'If you intend to go on with this case I can only say that there are higher authorities to whom I will protest most strongly.'

" 'You cannot threaten this court,' said the Magistrate.

"When Bere asked Superintendent Fitzpatrick when such a claim for costs was last made, the Magistrate said: 'That is irrelevant. Don't answer that.'

"Bere replied: 'That is not irrelevant. English law is being used as an instrument of political persecution.' "

In retrospect, at a distance of many years, there is an obviously humorous aspect to the bare details of this and similar courtroom scenes involving the young Republicans, however great the importance and seriousness of these issues to them at the time.

In the event, most costs and fines (with the exception of those of Tom and Joyce Williams in the Aberdâr case, for which they themselves took over responsibility) were met by the generosity of the many contributors to the Assistance Fund, of which mention is made in a later chapter.

Chapter 7

But the most important event of the year 1950 in the story of the Welsh Republican Movement was the publication in Eisteddfod week of the first issue of *The Welsh Republican — Y Gweriniaethwr*, the Movement's printed newspaper.

That this publication was to run for 41 consecutive issues, at two monthly intervals over a period of seven years is tribute enough to the success and appeal of its reading matter. Its first editor was Huw Davies, with Harri Webb active behind the scenes as Managing Editor.

The paper became the chief medium of WRM propaganda, and achieved a fairly consistent circulation approaching 2,000 for the first three years of its life. That circulation came to be divided eventually between some 300 and more postal subscribers (their names recorded for posterity), a 100 or so distributed for publicity purposes, some few dozen sold through the retail trade, and the remainder sold through personal contact in the pubs and on the streets, and sometimes from door to door.

The contents of No. 1 of Vol. 1 of this historic publication for Wales set forth the broad pattern of resolute, full-blooded political journalism which it was to follow throughout the seven years of its eventful life. This excerpt from the noteworthy first editorial sets the pace:

> "We will attack all forces threatening the national interest, the social, moral and economic welfare, or the territorial integrity of Wales and the Welsh People. We will expose the indignities and injustices to which our people are subjected due to their being deprived of political sovereignty. We will, at all times, encourage those citizens of our country who manifest their love for Wales by fearless action in the interests of Welsh sovereignty. Our inspiration will come from the saga of Welsh endeavour through the centuries. Our aim will be to steel the will of our people for the reconquest of Wales for a free and independent Welsh people, for the establishment of the Sovereign Independent Democratic Republic of Wales.
>
> "We invite the support of all the friends of Wales throughout the world to this, the voice of Welsh resistance to alien authority. We

warn those who would deny to our people the moral responsibility and the pressing social and economic necessity of national sovereignty, to stand aside. Wales must live; Wales SHALL live.

"Our first number is honoured by an article from a Scots writer of international renown, and by greetings from men whose leadership means much to the resurgent Celtic peoples. Our feature article, a striking exposure of the distortion of history so widely prevalent in the so-called 'education system' which is forming the ways of future generations of Welsh Citizens, gives us another important message. If Wales is to live, our people must know the Truth — about the past and present of our country. The whole fabric of falsehood by means of which the subordination of Wales to England is perpetuated, will be one of the main objects of the unceasing indictment of the present English order in Wales, to be conducted by *The Welsh Republican*."

"Korea. We Serve Neither King Nor Kremlin", a trenchant survey by Ithel Davies of the situation threating a new international conflict over Korea, takes its appropriate place on the front page, together with a report by Cliff Bere of a personal investigation made into the position of the forty six farmers and their families in the upper reaches of the Tywi Valley threatened with an annihilating take-over of their 20,000 acres of farmland by the English Forestry Commission. After his visit to the area three members of the Abertawe branch of the Movement, Ithel Davies and Tom and Joyce Williams, accepted an invitation from Mr D. Williams of Troed-y-rhiw, Rhandirmwyn, to visit his farm when many of the farmers would be there to help with the sheep shearing.

In the mellow light of evening after work with the sheep was over the three Republicans addressed the assembled farmers to great effect. Two or three of the farmers also spoke. As a result, the meeting passed an unanimous resolution that, come what may, they would never yield up their land, and that they were prepared to take positive, if not punitive, action against the Forestry Commission if it persisted in its plans.

That the determination so fiercely expressed by the farmers on this occasion was duly taken note of by the Forestry Commissioners could help to explain the favourable outcome for the farmers at the subsequent Inquiry into the Upper Tywi Compulsory Purchase Order.

And at the Inquiry itself, the Republicans were present too, and as the WRM's own record of the occasion was justifiably proud to be able to say: "Intervention by Abertawe members at the Tywi afforestation Inquiry was most successful, and drew widespread attention."

Also on the front page is room for a telling reprimand by the Editor, Huw Davies, under the title "Eisteddfod 'Frenhinol' ynteu Eisteddfod

Genedlaethol?" aptly summed up in the words of its final paragraph: "Chwi Eisteddfodwyr pybyr! Mynnwch ddiwedd ar y fath wrthuni gwacsaw ac estronol. Nid oes angen nawdd y frenhiniaeth Seisnig ar Ŵyl Genedlaethol ein Gwerin anorchfygol ni. Galwer yr ŵyl yn Eisteddfod Genedlaethol Cymru."

The feature article referred to in the editorial as 'a striking exposure of the distortion of (Welsh) History' is by Dr Ceinwen H. Thomas. And on the last page is the first of a notable series from the pen of Harri Webb — 'A Letter to Mr Jones'. And alongside it, the first of what was to be an equally notable, but perhaps somewhat more aggresive, sequence — 'Guilty Men'.

The first number of *The Welsh Republican* was printed by Adro Ltd., Cardiff.

★ ★ ★

Herbert Morrison, a prominent member of the Labour government, which had retained power, but by a very reduced margin, after the general election of 1950, provided, like his fellow Cabinet Minister, Emmanuel Shinwell, another unhappy example of a politician seduced by the taste of power from whatever may once have been sincere socialist and democratic ideals.

Herbert Morrison's oft expressed ambition whilst in government was to see the population of the Island of Britain boosted to 70 million and more in number, contrary to any balanced, objective, sane assessment of the adverse social and economic consequences that could ensue from such congestion. The Republicans had often stressed the importance of encouraging a reduction in the population of overcrowded Britain to a figure of about half its number of 50 or so millions. In a poll organized by the London *Daily Express* in 1948 some 48% of people polled were said to be prepared to emigrate to English-speaking lands overseas if financially assisted by the government. Obviously, Mr Morrison had found that the mantle of empire could sit not too uncomfortably on his shoulders, after all!

In October 1950 he came to address a very large gathering at the Plaza cinema hall in Abertawe. In the audience were three Republicans who had come to greet him. One by one, after their prolonged, repeated greetings, they were forcibly ejected from the hall. But leaflets in abundance had been scattered in the lower auditorium; and, before the last Republican was removed, in a great shower from the gallery.

They were not scattered in vain, for, according to *The Western Mail* report of the occasion, Herbert Morrison had one of the leaflets brought to him, and, very obligingly from the Republican protestors' viewpoint, decided to read it out to the packed assembly.

"Warning to Herbert Morrison, arch plotter against Wales," it read.

"The tide of Welsh freedom is rising.
No cockney Canute can turn it back.
Go back to plot in Putney.
Your Council for Wales is a fraud and a flop.
You deny the rights of Wales.
You have no right to speak in Wales.
Taw Sôn Sais.
(Printed and published by The Welsh Republican Movement)"

★ ★ ★

The next, the October-November, issue of *The Welsh Republican* contained an announcement expressing regret over the delay of some weeks in publication, which suggested an interesting, perhaps almost inevitable, little story as the reason for that delay, which was as follows.

In seeking for more favourable terms for the printing of the paper, a firm of printers in Tonypandy was contacted, and a quotation of £15-10-0 was received from them, with promise of delivery by the 2nd of October. This was accepted.

On return of the corrected proofs to them, however, the printers replied to say that they were not prepared to carry through the printing as they considered some of the contents to be 'defamatory and libellous' — an opinion they claimed, by their printing Assocation, and this in spite of a 'certificate of legality' requested by them at the outset of negotiations and which had been duly supplied by Mr Ithel Davies, barrister-at-law.

On the 10th of October there was a letter from the firm to the effect that they were prepared to "sell you the type as already set, if you can get another firm to undertake the printing and thereby helping you to get this issue in circulation. After the advice given to us we are not prepared to incriminate ourselves in any way."

In the upshot, it was the gallant firm of Gwasg Gee, Dinbych, who came to the rescue and agreed to print; and the type as set was despatched to them by rail from Tonypandy. (It was Gwasg Gee who helped to set the Republican bandwagon rolling by printing the first and second editions of Bere's *The Welsh Republic*).

The total amount of Gwasg Gee's bill for printing 2,000 copies was £10-9-0, which included the cost of returning the print by goods train and also the postage for direct despatch of a total of 850 copies of the paper between the following destinations:

150 . . . Pedr Lewis, Y Felinheli. 150 . . . Ifor Wilkes, Bangor.
100 . . . Cyril Huws, Coleg y Brifysgol, Aberystwyth.

  100 . . . Y Mri. W.H. Smith & Son, Station Road, Llanelli.
  150 . . . Tom Williams, Abertawe.
  200 . . . Glyn Thomas, Secretary, Cilelai Miners' Lodge, Tonyrefail.

  No. 2 of Vol. 1 was thereby enabled to be in circulation by the first days of November after a delay of a month, but which without the valued help of Gwasg Gee might have been considerably longer.

  This difficulty over the printing of the second issue of *The Welsh Republican*, as concerning the Tonypandy printers, was finally settled in July 1951 with a payment to them (in face of their claim for almost double the amount) of £5-1-0, being the difference between their original quotation of £15-10-0 and Gwasg Gee's bill of £10-9-0.

★ ★ ★

  The Republicans had already held meetings in the Rhondda, at Tonypandy on the 20th May 1950, where the union flag was burnt on Pandy Square, and in Porth and Treorci during the same period. They were also present at the Cilelai (*Cilely*) Colliery, Tonyrefail on 14th October that year as the pitcage was hauled to the surface shortly after 9 a.m., signifying the end of a stay-down strike when 62 miners were in the pit for over two days in protest at the proposed closing of the colliery. "Republican leaflets", ran a headline in a press report of the occasion. "At a pithead meeting before the men went home, which was addressed by Mr Bryn Williams, Lodge Chairman, a woman distributed leaflets assuring the miners of the support of the Welsh Republican Movement. The meeting ended in the singing of the Welsh National Anthem." And in implementation of that Republican assurance the front page spread of the October-November 1950 issue of *The Welsh Republican*, under the heading 'Threat to the Rhondda — London decides Cilely closure', gave an eloquent and penetrating analysis by Glyn Thomas, Cilelai Lodge Secretary, of the rank injustice in social and economic terms to be perpetrated upon the community of Tonyrefail. (This was possibly the first time in Welsh Nationalist journalism for a strike leader to state his case in an organ of the nationalist movement).

  "Suddenly out of the blue came the decision to close Cilely," wrote Glyn Thomas. "Around Cilely, and in particular Cilely Lodge over the years there has been built up a community of interests, Cilely being the hub, and radiating from it spokes into many and diverse local activities. At the moment one of the active Lodge members is busy erecting a social centre for the Old Age Pensioners of Edmondstown, to which the Lodge has given active support. We, jointly with a neighbouring Lodge, run the Tonyrefail Silver Band

> (and it is said the other Lodge has only five years life). We contribute to, and take an active part in the running of The Rhondda Institute for the Blind, and so on; in practically every phase of local life the Lodge is interested. To destroy such a community must demand a powerful case. What is that case? . . . The Lodge says the reserves are at least double, if not treble, the figures given by the (Coal) Board in their memorandum for closure; figures of 17 million and 20 million (tons) have been mentioned in previous meetings at pithead level. It would be interesting to know what were the figures of reserves, and the development plans, upon which the NCB are paying compensation to Powell Duffryn for Cilely Colliery. But even accepting the Coal Board's figures, we say it is a crime against the nation that 7 million tons of one of the finest steam coals should be lost to the nation for ever."

And what a portent of the unending succession of such socially and economically disastrous occasions to follow through succeeding decades was Cilelai to be!

'What is a Welshman?' was the headline above a short but very relevant item on page 2 of the October-November paper:

> "It is not merely someone born in Wales of Welsh blood. Such a person may renounce his nationality by acting in a manner inconsistent with it.
>
> "A Welshman is a citizen of Wales who — no matter what his race or language or country of origin — contributes to this country's welfare, maintains its best traditions and defends its rights and interests.
>
> "We refuse to accept any other definition.
>
> (This adaptation from the 'Scots Socialist' is gratefully acknowledged.)"

It is followed by an article headed 'Policy Discussion — No. 1. The Republic of Wales' and set out in two parts. Under the first sub-heading 'Why?' Ithel Davies writes:

> "We repudiate the entire thesis of monarchy as alien to every democratic and socialist principle. To us, sovereignty rests in the people of Wales expressed in and functioning through the political institutions native to, and fashioned by, them. It is of vital importance to the people of Wales that their allegiance shall be where their sovereignty is, in themselves as a political community. It is of vital importance to any national group. It is in that way they derive the inspiration and pride of their national being. It is in that way that they will realize their equality with all other free peoples of the world . . . in that way they will be able to co-operate effectively for the common

good of our common humanity across all borders and frontiers."

Under the sub-heading 'How?' Gwilym Prys Davies writes:

"In the founding of the Welsh Republican Movement — in the face of misrepresentation and money power, and without aid from the 'great Welshmen' of our age — the first stage in the political regeneration of our people has been accomplished. The second stage in the process of re-birth of our nation is for the citizens of Wales to accept and support our Movement so that we may march forward in their name to wrest from our exploiters that which is by eternal right our own. The third and final stage will be the founding and consolidation of the Independent Sovereign Republic of Wales.

"But the final stage will not be accomplished by an over-night manoeuvre; it will demand from all of us a determined effort spread over three, four or even five decades. Let there be no sweet illusion in our ranks. The strife will last many, many years, and we shall have to fight every inch of the way."

And in the flourish of the promise at the end of his second 'Letter to Mr Jones', Harri Webb under his pen name 'Caradog' writes:

"You are going to hear a different story from us, the Welsh Republicans. We're going to tell you that a Welshman should listen to nobody who tells him that he has no right to run his own country or be loyal to his own Welsh flag and who stuffs him up with a lot of rubbish about the Union Jack, which is an insult to Wales. And if the 'courts' come down on us and make us out to be criminals, remember that they are English courts, that they take their orders from over the border and their laws come from English statute books. Is that justice, Mr Jones? Just think it over.
       Yours truly,
       Caradog."

Chapter 8

On Saturdays in the Autumn and Winter of 1950 the Republicans spoke on the streets of Abertyleri, Tredegar, Glyn Ebwy (*Ebbw Vale*), Casnewydd (*Newport*), Bryn-mawr, and Y Barri. The Square in Y Bryn Mawr became a favourite venue for them; the meetings there always seemed to attract a good and appreciative crowd of listeners. The Republicans were not usually in a position to provide their own transport to these quite distant destinations, but almost invariably, despite the cost in time and money of the long bus journeys, they would return to their home base with a feeling of satisfaction over a mission accomplished.

And by now, of course, they had the further motivation of being able to take with them a supply of their very saleable Welsh Republican newspaper. There were occasions when after a meeting, as many as 150 copies of the paper would be sold on the streets and, in particular, in the pubs later in the evening.

But Republican activities were not concentrated solely on outdoor campaigning. Disruptive tactics at the indoor meetings of reneging politicians were part of their stategy. At this time, the Labour Party was still in government. The landslide victory at the 1945 General Election had been followed by a more modest success in 1950. But Labour gave not the slightest indication of being ready to redeem the promise of its policy of pre-war days of self-government for the Celtic nations of Britain. In respect of being prepared to acknowledge and give recognition to the identity of Cymru as a nation with the historical and inalienable right to govern itself, the rule of Labour government from London was still no different from that of any Tory government.

There are memories of more than one fierce clash at the old Cory Hall, Caerdydd — of a sleeker Jim Callaghan, M.P. of five or six years standing, attending there to share the platform with government Minister John Strachey at a Labour Party rally. And somewhere in *The Western Mail* photo archives there are known to be graphic unpublished shots taken on another occasion in that Hall, of Republicans caught in the process of being violently ejected from the gallery.

Perhaps George Thomas too, has memories of similar confrontations in the fittingly more modest venue of a school hall, perhaps, or meeting-room somewhere in Grangetown or other City district.

The Republicans in the North, and elsewhere, being without the number of members available in the South for militant activities, were, for the time being, mainly engaged in spreading the Republican message by word of mouth and through the sale of *The Welsh Republican* and other literature.

★ ★ ★

The No. 3, Vol.1 of *The Welsh Republican*, the December 1950 — January 1951 issue came out on time. It was printed by Messrs Brook & Williams of High Street, Y Barri, the firm which printed the paper throughout the remaining six and a half years of its publication. It is forgotten how exactly the Movement was first brought into contact with this firm (a fair surmise would be that it was through the diligent questing of the admirable Huw Davies); but for the whole of that period the paper came safely and almost always promptly from the press, and this in spite of, on more than one occasion, threats and personal visitations made to the printers by public figures alleging unjustifiable impugnment in its columns. To Mr Ken Jones, the firm's resolute proprietor in those and later days, Welsh Republicans continue to owe a debt of gratitude.

This issue of the paper was notable for the constructive and forward-looking front page article by Ithel Davies concerning leasehold tenure as it affected Welsh homes. The editorial of Huw Davies presented his usual fine analysis of events. Under the title "Make the Valleys Green — An Answer to the 'Dust' ", Cliff Bere suggested an obvious allocation for afforestation. And the inimitable Caradog penned his third 'Letter to Mr Jones'.

But pride of place must go to Huw Davies' half-column on the front page entitled 'Dinasyddion Cymru — Cymry ydym oll!'

> "Peth trist oedd darllen ysgrif yn y 'Cymro' beth amser yn ôl yn disgrifio gwaith y Cynghorydd Llewelyn Jenkins ar Gyngor Dinas Caerdydd. Cyfeiriwyd at Mr Jenkins fel 'yr unig Gymro' ar Gyngor Dinas Caerdydd. 'Saeson' oedd y Cynghorwyr eraill i gyd, yn ôl yr ysgrif. Ystyr 'Cymro' yma, wrth gwrs, yw Cymro sy'n siarad Cymraeg. Defnyddir y gair yn yr ystyr gul hon byth a hefyd gan 'garedigion y Gymraeg'. *Yr arfer hon yw un o'r pethau mwyaf peryglus yng Nghymru heddiw. Oni wêl ein Cymry Cymraeg y cam a wnânt â'u cyd-ddinasyddion? Oni welant y maen tramgwydd y maent yn ei roi yn llwybr undod ein cenedl?* Y mae pawb sy'n byw'n barhaol yng Nghymru yn Gymro. Y mae gennym yng Nghymru Gymry Cymraeg, Cymry di-Gymraeg o dras Gymreig, a Chymry di-Gymraeg o dras

anghymreig. Os dymunwn 'oes y byd' i'n hiaith rhaid i bawb yng Nghymru barchu'r Gymraeg fel ei etifeddiaeth ei hun, hyd yn oed os na fedr ef ei siarad. Nid mater o 'gadw'r iaith' i'r etholedig rai, yw hi bellach, ond mater o uno pob dinesydd Cymreig yn yr ymgyrch i greu cenedl Gymreig o'r elfennau gwahanol sydd gennym. Felly yr adferir y Gymraeg yn y parthau y ciliodd hi ohonynt. Felly y datblygir undod cenedlaethol. *Da chwi, Gymry sy'n siarad Cymraeg, peidiwch â rhoi sarhad ar fwyafrif ein cenedl drwy eu galw'n Saeson.*
Gol."

In January 1951 a branch of the Movement was established in Aberteifi (*Cardigan town*) under the leadership of Wynne Selby.

* * *

In the early Spring of 1951 there was an exciting time at a meeting near the railway station in Casnewydd (*Newport, Gwent*) when Huw Davies, who was speaking, came under physical threat from a strange character, enormous in physical stature, incongruously wearing old-fashioned clogs on his feet and blessed with a strident cockney accent, whose preliminary assault was launched in terms of the ripest of obscene language. Huw was saved from any impending physical hurt, when his Republican comrades countered the man's aggressive intent with their own show of counter aggression. And the situation was further relieved by the entry upon the scene of the landlord of a nearby pub calling on the man to 'give the boys a chance — come and have a pint' — which generous collaborative gesture was all that was needed to draw the man away and allow Huw to continue his speech to a by now well-augmented audience.

From this period too, there is remembered the occasion when members of the branches in the South came together for a joint meeting in front of the Abertawe Guildhall. Something that stands out in the memory of that event was a fine, fiery oration by the then Mair Saunders Lewis.

On the occasion of every such meeting now, *The Welsh Republican — Y Gweriniaethwr* had come to establish itself as an almost essential part of the proceedings, the presence of its written word lending added force and conviction to the message of the speakers. In the February-March 1951 issue Dr D.J. Davies of Pantybeiliau, Gilwern, economist and author of valuable publications in the cause of Welsh self-government, castigates the Labour government on its decision to create that behemoth of centralized immensity, the Margam steelworks, and thereby bringing unemployment to some 30,000 workers in the long-established West Wales tin-plate and steel industries. And much else he had to say could be fairly summed up in his final words:

"Is it not time that Welsh socialists learnt their lesson and abandoned their bogus internationalism and instead remember that they too have a country (that if they give Wales her chance, Wales will give them theirs)? So that out of a true love of their own country and service to her they can achieve a real internationalism and a readiness to co-operate as a nation with the other nations of the world."

In discussing the Parliament for Wales Campaign set up at Llandrindod in the previous year, and its projected Petition 'praying' the 'Honourable' House of England's Parliament to promote an act to set up a 'Parliament' in Wales, the Editor comments:

"True though the 'prayer' may be to the forms of English constitutional usage, these are not the accents of Welsh national leadership. Our nation, the Welsh Nation, does not need to speak like a stage Chinaman . . . Sincere patriots have acclaimed the Petition as a step towards National Unity . . . But," the incisive comment goes — *"National Unity is the product, not the prerequisite, of a National Freedom Movement."*

And the wise voice of Huw Davies is heard again when in giving welcome to the appearance of the Welsh Dictionary of the University of Wales from the University Press, he says:

"Ac, yn wir, y mae galw hefyd am eirfa dechnegol safonol. Ni ellir gorbwysleisio'r angen am wneud y Gymraeg yn gyfrwng digonol i holl bywyd diwydiannol cyfoes. Dyna amod ail-ennill i'r Gymraeg safle iaith y genedl gyfan. Ac ail-ennill y safle hwnnw yw amod parhad a datblygiad y Gymraeg i'r dyfodol."

In this issue, under the heading 'Wales and the World', appears the first of several subsequent articles by the redoubtable John Legonna, 'Keeper of the Celtic Conscience'. And too, Dr Jac L. Williams is given good space to put forward his controversial views concerning a place for the English language in the National Eisteddfod.

Under the title 'We believe in the Welsh People', Harri Webb writes:

"The common people are Wales; that is why, in 'The Century of the Common Man', Wales is coming to the forefront and may well play a part that will redeem all the humiliations of the past."

And so later in the same piece in prophetic vein he can write:

"But if the Welsh people are slow to convince, they can be sudden to convert, and history moves fast."

And that faithful, unremitting correspondent Caradog ends his 'Letter to Mr Jones' with the answer to that most pertinent of questions:

"The answer to the question 'Who runs Wales?' is this: *Everybody except the People of Wales.* Everybody who is willing to take his orders from the London money-men and the Whitehall office wallahs; English spivs and Welsh boot-lickers. Every body except *YOU*, Mr Jones.

Best wishes and happy dreams,
(You'll need them)
from Caradog."

Dr Thomas Jones, C.H., is the subject of Spy's column in this issue. It is reproduced here because no history of the Welsh Republican Movement could be complete without being ready to record the full measure of every aspect, constructive or destructive as occasion demanded, of its uncompromising political attitudes.

'Guilty Men' by Spy
No. 3 Dr Thomas Jones, C.H.

"Before the career of Thomas Jones, criticism is respectfully dumb. The Recording Angel has doubtless written that it was Thomas Jones who stood by with a hymn book while his master, Lloyd George, bloodily partitioned Ireland, that it was Thomas Jones who played a huge, if hidden, part in 'fixing' the Welsh-led and Welsh-inspired General strike of 1926, who gave his support to the Mond-Turner 'industrial truce' that made Wales a desert, and who watered the desert with his crocodile tears; that it was Thomas Jones who was 'unofficial Secretary for Wales' in a period when the people were being exported like cattle. It is not for us to chronicle these unforgettable achievements. We prefer to dwell on the wisdom of the philosophy that has inspired them. Hear it:

'Dear as Wales is to us there are some things that are dearer to us . . . If we are forced to make a choice we shall fight . . . for the British Commonwealth.' 'No disease can compete in destructiveness with the idea of . . . nationalism . . . To be willing to die for such an idea in Wales today is a gratuitous sacrifice to mental anarchy.' 'The idea that there are in England a lot of able Welshmen eager to return to Wales . . . is moonshine.' 'The only safety for small nations is to join a convoy.' (Like Korea perhaps?!)

Let us crown this selection with a further masterpiece of cynicism: 'The Welsh are a credulous nation and anything which can be dressed up as idealism has a fatal attraction for them.'

This is hardly fair though. Much as he may fear them, ideals have never had the chance to be fatal to Dr Thomas Jones, Companion of English Honour."

***

On Sunday the 18th of February 1951 in answer to the threat of the spread of war across the world again, members of the Labour Party, the Communist Party, Co-operative organizations, trade union branches and religious and many other bodies joined in the struggle to maintain peace by convening at four great conferences held in Caerdydd, Liverpool, Glasgow and London respectively. Representatives of a quarter million Welsh people came together at the Welsh Conference in the Cory Hall, Caerdydd. Ninety delegates attended from 44 trade union branches, including 34 lodges of the National Union of Mineworkers, and two delegates from the 90,000 strong Southern Wales area of the NUM.

A seven-point resolution was unanimously carried calling on the common people of all Nations and States to reach out towards one another in friendship to build up in the world an irresistible will to peace.

At the start of the Conference the 200 or so delegates and more than 300 visitors stood to sing 'Hen Wlad fy Nhadau'.

The Chairman of the Conference was Mr Ithel Davies of the Welsh Republican Movement. "We are gathered here," he said in his speech from the Chair, "to tell the government in London that Wales is finished with their wars, and that if there were another one they would have more trouble in Wales than they ever had in Ireland . . . We will organize public opinion in Wales so that the world may know where Wales stands. We have a right to be heard as a people."

"Dr R. Tudor Jones, Professor of Theology at Bangor University," said a press report, "spoke objecting to the use of Christ as 'a mascot at the head of the armies of Christendom', and objecting too, to Welsh blood being spilt in England's quarrels . . . A small country like Wales cannot afford to be involved in another war. I will say more — most Welshmen will not engage in another war."

Mr S.O. Davies, M.P. for Merthyr Tudful, who was unable to attend, had sent a telegram — "Do urge all delegates to work for peace. Britain dangerously drifting into war."

A widely representative Welsh National Peace Council was set up.

On the face of it, as a result of this important gathering, with Ithel Davies in the key rôle as Chairman, the Welsh Republican Movement was set fair to find nothing but political advantage accruing. But that was not to be. The event provided, on the contrary, a quite considerable setback for the Movement.

The writer of these records happened to be out of Cymru at the time of the Conference. Returning, he had seen reports in the press and heard accounts of some apparently brief but heated disturbance during its proceedings. It seemed that one or two well-known Republican members from the Abertawe area had interrupted with militant sentiments in terms quite inappropriate, politically and otherwise, for such a meeting.

Ithel Davies felt so compromised in the circumstances with which he had been faced, and in general so badly about the matter, that, in spite of earnest beseeching from all sides, he had by the end of March withdrawn his membership of the Council of the Movement. And apart from an occasional article in *The Welsh Republican* he took little further part in the Movement's activities.

It seems ironic that anything in the nature of an accusation of lack of militancy in the cause of his nation's freedom to decide for itself should ever have been levelled at a man such as Ithel Davies, who had heroically endured three years of harsh imprisonment and persecution for his patriotic ideals in resisting conscription into the insane slaughter of the 1914-18 war.

But, putting this regrettable incident behind them, the youth of the Movement kept their eyes turned to the future.

On the 28th of April the Abertawe branch of the Movement were in Creunant. "Welsh socialists cannot expect an imperialist country like England to accept and put into practice in its political system the ideas and principles that we in Wales have always cherished," said Tom Williams in an effective speech. "That is why the faith of a man like Aneurin Bevan can eventually end in ineffectuality and frustration. He finds, though he does his best to take on the mantle of an Englishman, that all he earns for his pains in the end is the hatred and dislike of the English." (What a lesson there could have been here for Welsh socialist politicians of a later day!) "We in Wales had been ready to believe that the English Labour Party was ready to accept the ideas of Welsh Socialism which are founded on and evolved from the social and humane ideals of Welsh social civilization. But now we in Wales have found to our cost that it is the English interpretation of things that has taken over in the Labour Party."

Joyce Williams directed her speech at what she called the insincerity and hypocrisy of those in Wales who declared that the essential basis of their patriotism was their pacifism. "Pacifism is an excellent and serviceable principle for the English, French, Russian and American protestors," she said. "But for us as Welsh patriots it is a dangerous, false and un-Welsh attitude."

Haydn Jones of Ynysmeudwy, Pontardawe spoke about the 46 farms in the Tywi Valley under threat from the Forestry Commission. "We in the industrial valleys must give them all our support in their stand for justice," he said. "It is to the bare slopes of our industrial valleys that afforestation plans must be directed. There would be no need to turn people from their farms and homes. It would bring alternative work in the clean air to men under threat from ill-health in their work underground. We in the Welsh Republican

Movement have brought our standpoint on this subject forcibly home to the English government."

Chapter 9

Towards the end of Spring 1951 there came signs that the police in their attitude to the WRM were beginning to be motivated by considerations that were more intrinsically political in nature than of being simple matters of law and order as such. As an open-air meeting held in Pontardawe on the 25th of May by members from the Abertawe area was proceeding, the police broke into the middle of the meeting to ask for the names of the speakers. Believing they were on safe ground for refusing the police request, the speakers duly refused to give their names. As if in surprise and by way of retaliation at their spirited stand, the police Inspector in charge blustered that he would see to it that the Welsh Republican Movement would no longer be allowed to hold meetings in the Abertawe area again, and gave as a specific reason for this the suspicion that it was the Republicans who were responsible for the recent defacing of the car of the Mayor of Abertawe with painted slogans.

A week later at a meeting on a fine Saturday evening near to Coney Beach in Porthcawl a lone policeman, who, it seems, had been summoned there by a perturbed English visitor, had felt obliged to send for police reinforcements. "The people were all across the pavement and the road. There were hundreds there, Sergeant," he was heard to say to justify his call for assistance. At the height of the meeting Harri Webb had referred to the four union flags on the nearby pavilion as "polluting the air above the fair land of Wales." Cliff Bere had said his piece. Huw Davies was getting into full swing when the police Sergeant arrived and took it on himself to order disbandment of the meeting. The Republicans took solace in a healthy sale of their newspaper.

On the 16th of June the Republicans were in Castell Nedd (*Neath*) to hold a meeting in the town centre not far from the spot where a year or so before they had first burned the imperial flag in public. The meeting had progressed for about three-quarters of an hour, with Joyce Williams, Huw Davies and Cliff Bere speaking before a considerable crowd of onlookers, when the police arrived in force, obviously determined to put an end to the proceedings. They quickly moved the body of the crowd away in spite of the fact that the site of the meeting was on a roadway closed to traffic.

The Inspector asked the speakers for their names. When they refused to give them because he would not say what purpose he had in asking for them, he threatened them with arrest unless the names were forthcoming. The Republicans gave names, and they they were asked to produce identity cards, which they told him they didn't have with them. They were ordered to produce them at their local police stations within 48 hours.

When the police had gone, two or three of the onlookers who were still on the scene tendered their names to the Republicans as witness to what they considered a quite unjustifiable interference by the police.

★ ★ ★

In the April-May 1951 issue of *Y Gweriniaethwr* Eoin Mahony, Irish patriot and Celtic ally, put forward this constructive idea in his front page article 'Free Wales — United Ireland':

> "Wales might well ask Ireland to foster trade between the two countries by appointing a career Consul in Cardiff and Swansea, and honorary Consuls in as many Welsh towns as have residents willing to act as Consuls and having at heart the promotion of trade between the two countries and having a knowledge of Welsh or Irish, or both. Some of these could be of Irish blood, but the vast majority should be Welsh people . . . All Consuls, honorary or career, should combine on Welsh and Irish National occasions in a manner worthy of Wales and Ireland."

The editorial of Huw Davies, in his invariably cogent style, dealt with "The re-armament programme of England's government and the legislation passed at Westminster to prepare manpower for the worldwide conflict which English leaders anticipate . . . "

On an inside page, 'A Welshman's Resolve' by a 'Z reservist who served in England's Eighth Army during the last war' declares:

> "If and when my call-up papers come I am going to put into practice the principle of another discipline. I mean the self-discipline which is the spirit of Welsh resistance. I am going to demonstrate *that* discipline against English military 'discipline'. I am going to prove to myself and all fellow Welshmen who once fought like me for England that the spirit of a Welshman is stronger than the chains of the English army."

'Guilty Man', No.5 on this occasion, is Sir J.F. Rees, M.A.,Ll.D., who had recently served on the Advisory Commission on Self-Government for Ceylon, but who, "as 'Welsh' member of the late-lamented English Local Government Commission . . . took sides approving proposals which *excluded* Monmouthshire from amongst the Welsh counties." The fact that this man had at the dinner of the Pembrokeshire Association a week or so before attacked the Movement in virulent terms gave added spice to this Republican riposte.

Caradog writes his 'Letter' — to *Mrs* Jones this time — in nostalgic vein:

> "And if you want to know what good the Welsh Republicans will do when it comes to your side of the business, then just take a look at your meat ration — and goodness knows what it will be down to by the time you get this letter. You'll have to agree, we couldn't do very much worse. And if you're old enough to remember Welsh mutton and Welsh ham and 'Welsh Produce', then you will have an idea of what you are being done out of."

But perhaps this issue of our paper was mostly notable for this commemoration of a brave Breton patriot:

> "It is our privilege to publish for the first time in any country a poem in translation, written in the prison of Rennes, Brittany, by *Leon Jasson*, a young Breton soldier who fought for Breton Independence during the last war. The force in which he served, the 'Brezen Perrot', was the first organized Breton Army for over 400 years. It was called after a Breton Priest, Father Yanni-Var Perrot who was murdered by the French Resistance Movement for his Breton Nationalism. Jasson was captured and sentenced to death by the French. This poem was written on the eve of his execution. He had left many other writings which it is hoped to publish in Wales shortly.
>
> > Let the first birds sing for us
> > The coming of the hour
> > When the heart of the bravest leaps:
> > To-morrow morning, my head high
> > I shall go, joyfully, at the hour
> > When the first birds sing.
> >
> > July 16th, 1946.
> > (Shot at dawn — 17th July 1946)"

★ ★ ★

A fairly obvious indication of the increasing notice the police were taking of the political aspects of Republican activities was in their attitude to our slogan painting. Throughout the past winter in particular, suitable, practicable sites had been adorned with the brief and potent slogan — 'WALES A REPUBLIC'. An attempt had been made at dire risk to life and limb upon the great railway viaduct (now demolished) carrying the Rhymni Valley — Barri line high above the Tâf Valley near Ffynnon Tâf (*Taff's Well village*).

Frustrated in that attempt, the slogan painters had succeeded in putting their slogan at the top of the 20ft or so high wall (also long demolished) on the approaches to the village.

The following night, Davies, Bere and Webb had made the journey there in curiosity to survey the handiwork. As they approached in the darkness along the main road they saw a light illuminating their slogan, and, a shadowy shape in front of it at the top of a high ladder, a policeman busily scrubbing. They walked on in silence past his supervizing sergeant standing at the foot of the ladder. (It was this wall of great length and height towering alongside the main roadway, that it was planned to bring down with explosives on the occasion of a planned journey of the English queen along that route some months later. The operation was not proceeded with, although all preparations had been made, it is understood, because of the proximity of a nearby domestic dwelling on the other side of the road).

It was, indeed, as if the words 'Wales a Republic' carried so potently subversive a message in the eyes of authority, that they could not be allowed to challenge the public gaze for a moment longer than it could take to delete them. That that same slogan on the wall of the old *Western Mail* building in Golate Lane and on the front facade of Caerdydd railway station should also come in for deletion by morning light was perhaps a little more acceptable.

During following years of Republican activity, 'Wales a Republic', almost wherever painted, seemed to draw the immediate erasing attention of the authorities.

But the zeal and youthful energy of the Republicans found expression in other directions too: for instance — a successful raid in Castell Caerdydd on a night in June 1951 during the period of a so-called Festival of Britain when the ramparts of the castle were ringed with a multitude of flags — with the flag of Cymru, instead of having pride of place, hardly to be discerned amidst that unseemly riot of imperial colour.

Two athletic members of the Movement had stayed in the castle grounds after the gates were locked, and hidden until darkness set in. Their target was to be as many of the offending imperial emblems as they could snatch from the ramparts and conveniently carry wrapped about their bodies. Their retreat was to be over the castle's rear wall looming high above the darkness of Bute Park. For this purpose they had taken in with them a rope purloined a few days before in the cause of Cymru from the flagpole of a well-known public corporation. The original rope, of great length but obviously inadequate to bear the weight of a human body, had been plaited together to give it treble strength.

At an appointed time and place in the darkness under the castle wall a welcoming crew waited to greet the returning raiders. Down came the end of the plaited rope; it hung a few feet short of the ground. Then, high above, appeared a shadowy figure preparing to descend. But no sooner did he seem to be on the rope, than down he came at breakneck speed, his foot striking a glancing but painful blow to the upturned face of Harri Webb. The main bodily damage that night, however, was to the hands of Arthur Watson, one of the bold raiders. The plaited rope, as soon as he had entrusted his weight to it, had sagged so alarmingly that he had thought it was breaking, and down he had come at hand-skinning speed.

He was duly followed by his companion of the night at a more leisurely pace down the rope by now initiated into weightbearing service.

★ ★ ★

On Sunday night, 24th June, Tom and Joyce Williams and others from the Abertawe branch addressed an open-air meeting of the Anti-partition Association in O'Connell Street, Dublin, near the GPO where the Republican HQ was established in 1916. The crowd gave them a memorable welcome. The importance of co-operation between Wales and Ireland became an important theme of the meeting, the Chairman saying: "Wales is our nearest neighbour. Any success gained by the Welsh Republicans is a nail in the coffin of English imperialism and brings the day of Irish Unity nearer."

★ ★ ★

Harri Webb was living at this time in rooms on the top floor of No. 39, Fitzhamon Embankment, Caerdydd. His landlady, Mrs Sobolewski, a native of Llangennech, was a pleasant young Welsh-speaking lady married to a Polish soldier or airman. When Cliff Bere's wife, Eluned, had to leave for Bala with her baby son to tend her ailing mother he had moved in to share the top floor accommodation with Harri Webb. There are a few amusing stories to be told of their stay together over a period of two or three months, but which are not strictly part of the story of the WRM. A visitor on one or two occasions was that former colleague of Harri, Keidrych Rhys (then resident in London), who played a small part in painting a slogan on Caerdydd railway station one night as he rushed to catch the London train.

That address near the centre of Caerdydd made a convenient rendezvous for fellow Republicans, and the roof guttering which was accessible from the top floor made a ready hiding place for different items from time to time in anticipation of visits from the police.

The Republican newspaper had attracted the notice and approbation of Sinn Fein, and London members of that Movement were in correspondence with the WRM. In July 1951, and also at a later date that year, one of them, Seán MacStíofáin, paid a visit to 39, Fitzhamon, bringing with him various items that he considered might be useful to the Welsh Republican cause. There were also visits from other London Sinn Feiners, made with the objective of promoting co-operation between the two Movements.

The correspondence with MacStíofáin continued for some time — until the Autumn of 1953, from outside prison, and then from inside, to where he had been remanded, jointly charged with the taking of several hundred rifles from an army stores in Felstead, Surrey. A letter from him from Brixton prison, dated 16th September 1953, says: "We go for trial in about three weeks time, on or after the 6th of October . . . It's hard to say what we will get, but I don't think it will be less than five years, and I don't think we will get more than seven years, but, as I say, it is hard to say . . . "

He got, in fact, eight years. From time to time for a year or two following his sentence the WRM was able to send a modest sum by way of financial help to his wife Mary in the south of Éire. (MacStíofáin was Chief of Staff of the Provisional IRA from 1970-72. He took a prominent rôle in the IRA — British Government talks in July of 1972).

★ ★ ★

"If England's Labour Party has failed this generation of the Welsh people," concludes the incisive editorial of the June-July 1951 *Gweriniaethwr*, "its betrayal of past and future Welsh generations is more complete. The perpetuation of our national popular heritage has been signally, if inevitably, neglected by so-called 'Labour'. It is the duty of the Welsh Republican Movement to produce the social enthusiasm and dynamic needed to establish the political sovereignty of the Welsh people in the immediate spiritual and material interests of this generation, and for the everlasting resurgence of the true life of Wales."

Under the heading 'Why there was no Welsh Army', a telling indictment on the front page offers the reason why, during the last war, Wales was denied the privilege shared by other allied nations 'from Belgium to Basutoland' in the fight against fascism.

Alongside is a brief insert headed 'Inflation', to warn that "rising costs force us to increase the price of your *Welsh Republican* (from 2d.) to 3d., beginning with the next issue." Oh, happy days!

Under 'Pryder yn Nhywi', Huw Davies reminds: "Mae'r Ymchwiliadau ynghylch y cynllun Seisnig i goedwigo Dyffryn Tywi yn parhau. Ers dwy flynedd bellach, y mae teuluoedd y ffermydd a fygythir yn byw mewn pryder beunyddiol."

'Guilty Man' No. 6 is levelled at "George Charles Henry Victor Paget, 7th Marquess of Anglesey, Earl of Uxbridge, educated at Wixenford, Wokingham and Eton (who) describes himself as 'a young Englishman'."

An article, 'Beat England's Planners', by Foelatt, a well-known authority in the field of electric power generation and transmission, states:

> "There is no sound technical reason why Wales should not be constituted an entity for the generation, transmission and distribution of electricity. Transmission lines will some day run North and South to give supplies of electricity to Central Wales . . . Wales is aroused and demanding the removal of the arbitrary 'electric fences' which divide the country."

On another page, under the title 'Wales must call the tune — The voice of true internationalism', Owen Owen says something that seems as significant, if not more so, today as it was in the very heyday of England's imperialist expansion: "English nationalism is the meanest form of nationalism, narrow and egotistical, and absolutely incompatible with any form of internationalism."

And Caradog's words of wisdom to Mr Jones have that so familiar ring of the naked truth, making them perhaps even more relevant today than they were when written: "Mr Jones, the reason is simply this: nobody in Wales has any responsibility at all. No decisions are ever allowed to be taken. The remote Ministries in London, who can't even pronounce the names of most places in Wales, make every decision of importance . . ."

★ ★ ★

The months of June and July 1951 had, indeed, their full complement of varied activities. A highly successful meeting in the centre of Pontypridd on the 7th July is well remembered. *Y Gweriniaethwr* sold effortlessly amongst the crowd whilst the oratory of Huw Davies and Harri Webb held them there listening. Members of the audience came forward to congratulate and thank the speakers. A member of the Communist Party who was present asked: "Why do the Republicans seem to have more appeal for the people of the Valleys than we Communists ever seem to have?"

And again, an equally successful meeting outside Merthyr Town Hall on Saturday evening 21st July stands out in the memory for the fiery eloquence of Webb in full flow and the admiration it evoked from his hearers.

But there was the occasional frustration, too. When the news came that Elizabeth, queen consort of England, was to make a ceremonial visit to Castell Caerdydd, the Republicans took due and careful note of official plans and preparations for the occasion. After the ceremony, Elizabeth was to leave the Castle by the rear entrance and cross into Bute Park via the wooden bridge over the dock-feeder canal. This was too good an opportunity to let go by, and it was decided to make a Republican commemoration of that royal occasion by destroying the bridge the night before the Castle ceremony. The necessary means to do that were available, having been carefully stored by two young women members in Ogmore Vale.

To do the job it was decided to call down a young member of the Movement from the Canolbarth (Mid-Wales) who would almost certainly be unknown to the police in the South. In the meantime, reconnaissance into Bute Park at night two days before the royal visit had not seen evidence of any security patrol in the park. The young man, Trefor Davies-Isaac by name, arrived, slightly nervous, although having no knowledge of exactly what he had been called down to do, but sensing that it was to be serious business, which he would be fully prepared to carry through.

A reconnaissance on the penultimate night, however, found that the park was now being patrolled. Perhaps that plaited rope left, of necessity, hanging from the Castle wall not far from the scene of the intended strike had given a reminder that there were 'unloyal subjects' at large.

The hard to conceal relief on that fine young face when told of the decision to abandon the operation is still remembered.

Another member who was active in the Movement at this time was John Normington, a native of Glyncorrwg, who had served for some years in the Merchant Navy. He was a fervent Welsh patriot, but, like so great a multitude of the people of Wales, had had to move to the English midlands to find work, where he met in Birmingham Delwyn and Lil Phillips, warm and generous supporters of the WRM.

John Normington was about 35 years of age when he came to stay for a short time in Caerdydd during the summer of 1951. With his athletic build and ability he performed feats of gathering in the alien imperial regalia flaunting itself on buildings and in public places. As a result, blankets, etc. in more than a few Republican homes were soon to be found hem-embroidered in red bunting.

Sadly, John Normington, model of a fine and fighting Welshman, died and was buried in England before his dream of coming home to Wales for ever could be realized.

★ ★ ★

In July 1951, Alfred Pocock, a gardener working in Llanfynydd and an active member of the WRM, was charged in court and fined a total of over £9, including costs, for refusing to fill in a 'national' census form; and in the following September suffered a short term of imprisonment in default of payment.

A few days later, on the 25th of July, Cliff Bere appeared before the Caerdydd Stipendiary Magistrate, Guy Sixsmith, on the same charge.

"I am a member of the Welsh Republican Movement," the press reported Bere saying in resisting the charge. "It is our intention to make a dead letter of English law in Wales. As a citizen of a free Wales I would give every assistance in completing the questionnaire required by a Welsh government. As far as England goes, she can ask in vain — until she is red, white and blue in the face.

"On being told by the prosecution that this was the only case of such a refusal in Cardiff, and one of only five in all of Wales, the Magistrate told Bere, 'I do not propose to make a martyr of you, and as it is such an insignificant number I do not think it calls for any strong action, so I will discharge you absolutely.' "

In September, Alfred Pocock, knowing he was to be arrested, wrote a letter as follows:

"To the Magistrates of the court of English Justice at Llandeilo, Wales. Why am I to be dragged before this so-called court of justice? That this flimsy charge has been persisted in is a matter of the greatest concern to the people of this district, and not only to them but to all respectable people everywhere. I suggest that the answer is simple. It is because I refuse to look upon the king of England as the anointed of Heaven and the English nation as the chosen of Heaven carrying out a heavenly inspired policy of might is right.

"Because I refuse to believe that all Welshmen are traitors and decline to oblige England in believing the Welsh constitution dead . . .

"I have already made my standpoint clear to you at the hearing of the case. As a Welsh Republican I refuse to recognise the authority of the law of England in Wales.

"In a similar case at Cardiff, the Stipendiary Magistrate saw fit to dismiss for some reason or other the case against another Welsh Republican without a fine. The Stipendiary Magistrate was an Englishman. Here at Llandeilo, before a Bench of Welshmen — the Chairman a man who professes to support Welsh culture and a man who attempts to be a leading figure in Welsh Nonconformist life, I was fined, and will, I have little doubt, be imprisoned.

"Of the 200 cases of people refusing to complete census forms throughout these islands, the English Registrar General stated that 20 were to be prosecuted. The number who refused to complete census forms in Wales was 5, yet all five have been prosecuted. Yet another example of English justice.

Long live Wales!
A. Pocock"

In July of the following year Alfred Pocock was to lose his job as a gardener because of his political convictions; they had come to the notice of his employer when he contested and won a seat on the Llanfynydd Parish Council.

Chapter 10

For some time, it had been the wish of Huw Davies, Bere and Webb, by now key figures in the Movement, to establish themselves in a more permanent, independent base from which they could more easily and effectively spread their political ideas amongst the people of the industrial valleys in the South.

In July 1951 an empty shop premises, No. 104, Gilfach Street, Bargoed in Cwm Rhymni had been offered on sale at a price of £1000. The Republicans went to have a look at it. As well as the shop space, there were four bedrooms in the premises, and quite adequate living accommodation behind the shop, with a large cellar underneath. It was a stone-built house of good appearance, with very little indication of damage from subsidence. But £1000, a quite substantial sum in those days, seemed well out of reach of the impecunious young Republicans — until, in a gesture of faith which he never had cause to regret and is still remembered for, Mr Edwards the owner, up to then completely unknown to the would-be purchasers, agreed to leave £700 of the sale price on mortgage of the premises.

The £350 or so necessary to complete the transaction was still something of a financial obstacle for the purchasers. This, however, was got over with the help of a most generous contribution of £100 from a prominent member of the Bangor based group of the Movement, Pedr Lewis. His name was duly incorporated into the deeds. But, so far as he can remember, it was only once that he ever set foot in those premises of his joint ownership, and that for a brief overnight stay.

The immediate preoccupation of the new owners in residence, who included Mrs Eluned Bere now happily able to return from the North with her baby son, was to put the establishment on as sound an economic basis as possible. Huw Davies continued in his employment as export sales executive with the firm of Cory Brothers in Caerdydd. The train service through Gilfach Halt a couple of hundred yards down the road was convenient, and he commuted daily to work.

Bere and Webb turned their attention to the empty shop to try to put in into use and make an economic proposition of it. Harri Webb's experience in the book trade seemed to supply the answer. 2,000 second-hand books were obtained for a few pounds from the sale of a small library further down the valley; Bere put his hand to shop-fitting; and a supply of paper-backs and children's books and stationery goods and similar items was ordered. The crowning touch to the launch of this new venture into the commercial life of Bargoed was the very impressive job made by a professional sign-writer from nearby Aberbargoed of the fascia board above the double-fronted shop — LLYFRGELL A SIOP LYFRAU BARGOED LIBRARY AND BOOKSHOP. And we were in business — or so we hoped.

★ ★ ★

The Welsh Republican for August-September 1951 was published from the Bargoed address. In the leading article, 'Capital for Wales — The Claim of Cardiff', Dr D.J. Davies put the case for the city to be given official recognition as a capital.

> "The possession of a capital has an important psychological effect upon members of the nation and outsiders. It gives recognition for the nation in the world at large . . . It wins for us the respect of and thereby engenders in us a sense of national self- respect . . . Today, more than ever, we need a capital, to begin the crystallisation of the national spirit . . . "

Under the title 'Why no Welsh Films?' Stewart Ainsley writes as if in prophecy:

> "In a free and independent Wales a Film Unit would add to Welsh culture. It would play a great part in returning the Welsh language to the priority it demands — giving it added richness and beauty; with grace and imagination it can tell its old tales — true stories of Welsh struggles for independence and liberty.
>
> "The film industry can help so much in giving us back the glory that we have lost under a nation that has been so cold — so hard — and never at peace."

Mae Huw Davies yn crynhoi ei sylwadau am 'Addysg Gymraeg' gyda'r geiriau: "Barnwn fod amgylchiadau'n galw ar ein hysgolheigion gwlatgar i weithredu yn hytrach nag i ddadansoddi." And his editorial is a telling critique of the aims and attitudes of the 'Parliament for Wales' campaign of that day.

In his article 'Our Country — Our Language' John Legonna disavows the inevitability of having to associate religious belief with the defence of the Welsh language.

> "The attitude of the Welsh Republicans to the Welsh language is substantially a political one," he says. "The Welsh language is an integral part of the Welsh national heritage: therefore it shall be

defended. The Welsh Republicans will at all costs refuse to allow that which countless generations of our forefathers have fashioned and handed down, to be jettisoned to the prevailing Anglo-Saxon megalomania . . . Our language is the symbol of our achievement: our cherishing of it is the badge of our pride in our nationality and of our appreciation of our inheritance. The language of Wales is as much the prize and honour of the sinner as the saint, of the agnostic as the Christian, of the idler as the man of serious intent."

In the back page spread, 'We Fight for Welsh Freedom — A Plague on Pacifism!', Mair Saunders Lewis begins:

" 'Nothing worthwhile can be won without suffering. Many more than I will go to prison and the scaffold before our freedom will be won.' These are the prophetic words spoken by James Connolly the great Irish Socialist before his execution after the Easter Rising in Dublin, 1916. How truly he spoke! It was only through bloodshed and imprisonment that Ireland gained her liberty . . . "

She ends by saying:

"The doctrine of Welsh Republicanism is one of responsibility and self-respect. We shall unite Wales in an aim and a purpose worthy of her illustrious past. Are we less brave than the Irish or the Jews? Are we less brave than our traditional enemy the English? They have shed their blood in the cause of England.

"Wales can only gain her freedom when we raise the Red Dragon rampant. We must forget our pacifist past. We must break the jaws of the Bulldog and march to freedom. Then, and only then will Wales rise again triumphant."

★ ★ ★

The move into the Bargoed HQ was for those concerned, perhaps a welcome respite from the round of political activities. For some weeks their efforts had to be mainly concentrated on more domestic matters. The furnishing of the house, as well as the shop, occupied their time and energies. The big bedroom over the shop was allocated for use as a political office, for WRM meetings, and so on, leaving the three other bedrooms, two small and one of family size, to provide comfortable sleeping accommodation.

Extending along the valley below the road, and cutting off any sight of neighbouring Aberbargoed the other side of the valley, loomed the great Bargoed tip of colliery spoil, reputedly one of the largest of such tips in Europe. Not far away, of course, in the valley bottom was the colliery with its power generating station nearby. Some months after their arrival in Bargoed the

Republicans had made their effort to initiate a tree-planting project on the slopes of the man-made mountain that formed their eastern horizon. Some years later, long after the Republicans had left Bargoed, this idea was carried into practical effect with the help of the pupils of local schools, and with very improving and pleasing results.

The problem of the fine, powdery dust expelled by the chimney stacks of the power station below also became the subject of Republican efforts to have something done to curb the resulting dirt and devastation endlessly carried on the wind onto and, in particular, under the slate roofs of Bargoed. A morning after a stormy night is remembered when on the way to Gilfach Halt the entire roadway was blue in the debris of shattered, rotted roof slates.

By merciful providence No. 104 Heol Gilfach had escaped almost unscathed. And mercifully too, in later years that problem at least ceased to inflict the citizens of Bargoed.

The Bargoed Republicans made use of this initial period of comparative relaxation whilst adjusting to their new environment, by helping to draw up reports, financial and otherwise, to set before the Annual General Meeting of the Council of the WRM later in the Autumn, and in general to bring up to date necessary paperwork and matters of organization — and to consider plans for the future. And of course the preparation of the next issue of *Y Gweriniaethwr* was always under consideration. The paper had by now become an important and stirring expression of Welsh national opinion, with the appearance of each issue coming to be looked forward to eagerly — with the exception perhaps, of certain public figures uneasy about catching the eye of Spy of 'Guilty Men'.

The distribution of the paper to postal subscribers had already become something of a task; the number of these subscribers, many of them prominent public figures, already exceeded 200, and eventually ran into a figure of more than 300.

The Assistance Appeal launched through the paper to help to keep defendants in the courts out of prison had reached a total of over £100 by mid 1951. Out of the names on the list of contributors, many of them well-known in the affairs of our nation, that of Ms B.O. Jones, Bradford House, Cwmllynfell, who sent what was in those days the very generous sum of £3, stands out somehow amongst them. She was entirely unknown in personal terms to the Republicans, but her name is well-remembered as a fervent patriot from her many letters in the columns of the press in those and later days.

There had been an encouraging increase in membership in the different branches, and in the Bangor area in particular, which was doing fine work in promoting the Republican cause via street and door to door sales of *Y Gweriniaethwr*.

It was later in the Autumn that the Bargoed establishment had its first visit from Rhydwyn Lloyd Pughe of Bryncrug, Tywyn, Meirion. He arrived on his powerful motor-bike to stay overnight. He might almost be said to have been an emissary from Gwilym Prys Davies, a close friend of his from early schooldays. Gwilym had been ill and through a lengthy period of convalescence and unable to take a very active part in WRM activities.

It was Rhydwyn who a year or so earlier had painted that long-enduring 'Freedom for Wales' slogan on the great wall of the Sir Gar council offices fronting on the Tywi bridge approach to Caerfyrddin town. In later years he held the office of Is-lywydd of Undeb Amaethwyr Cymru (Deputy President of the Farmers Union of Wales). He died on the 21st of May 1991.

* * *

Although the Bargoed address was now to all intents and purposes the operative HQ of the WRM, with Huw Davies and Harri Webb, Editor and Managing Editor respectively of the Movement's newspaper both resident there, it was decided to return to the use of a Cardiff address as the paper's official place of publication. The idea behind this was undoubtedly that publication from a city rather than a small valley-town address would reflect better from the aspect of prestige and credibility on the paper as the organ of the Welsh Republican Movement. The securing of a Caerdydd address presented no difficulty; but whether or not the move was well-founded in reason, it was then and still is difficult to decide.

On the front page of the October-November 1951 issue under the heading 'Sail yr Ymerodraeth' there is quoted:

"*Tri enw ym mhedryfan byd y rhoddir ar a ddyco eiddo arall: anrheithiwr, carnlleidr, a Sais (O Lyfr Trioedd Beirdd Ynys Brydain, casgliad 1650)*",

in succinct justification of the uncompromising policy and steadfast purpose of the WRM.

The realist words of Ifor Huws Wilkes on page 3 echoed that same truth in the broader setting of that later day:

"In the sphere of 20th century politics, Welsh Republicanism must secure the backing of a united people, of miner and quarryman, of docker and landworker. Nor must our sphere of action be limited by any narrow racial impositions; the Arab from Tiger Bay is our concern, equally with the Welsh speaker from the Cefngwlad. All that we demand is that both shall be prepared to accept the duties of citizenship in a Welsh State. Without them, all our national aspirations must remain an empty phantasm of cultural autonomy for those who cherish the abstract ideal more than the living people. Only our complete independence from the English Crown can prevent Wales being dragged at the end of an imperial leash into that insane maelstrom of power politics that understands only the argument of the atom-bomb."

And again, the challenge of the author of *The Welsh Republic* on that same page must strike perhaps with even greater relevance into the scenario of this a still later day:

" 'There is a tide in the affairs of men . . . '

"So too in the affairs of nations. And there is not a man or woman of the awakening generation in Wales who does not feel, whether by instinct or by reason, that the turn of the tide is at hand for the Welsh nation.

"For centuries Wales has lain in the backwaters, inert, a helpless, almost aimless, witness of the world's events. Only spasmodically and without coherence have there been signs of that force which would push her out again on to the moving waters. By today however there is already behind us a quarter century of sustained and multiplying evidence of the national resurgence. Wales is beginning to move again, however slowly, into the stream of events.

"It is vital however for us to guard against the idea that from here on the story of Wales's emancipation is to be one of a gradually increasing but orderly tempo of affairs as a result of labour, self-sacrifice and patience rewarded, until at last she is able to sail unmolested and in perfect trim into the path of freedom. *Our freedom will not come like that. The tide that is to bear Wales will rise suddenly. It will snatch her headlong from where she rocks at gentle rebellion into the fury of the storm.*

"The message of the Welsh Republican Movement to Wales is that she should be ready to face the change in the pace of events; and that she should be ready to take advantage of events when they happen, to the uttermost. For the tide that rises so quickly for Wales will be the tide that recedes for England. It is with the disintegration of the economic and political system of England under which they live that the Welsh people will come to see with increasing self-confidence the right and the necessity of their own political salvation.

"The watchword is 'Be Ready!' For the imperial veneer which has so long invested England's system of living with the appearance of stability is already being stripped away. We must be ready to face England minus the mask of civilization which she has worn so long. For the England that sees herself slipping into ruin will be the England of blood and iron and the cry of consolidation at any cost. It is the fate of the Welsh people to face this. It is their destiny to overcome it."

Chapter 11

The coming of Autumn 1951 saw the flexing of Republican muscles and vocal chords to face the challenge of a new season with its growing portents of change in the political set-up.

The Bargoed crew, the process of settling into their new home satisfactorily accomplished and having played their part in the organization of the Movement's formal business affairs, were impatient to get on with the work of carrying the Republican message out from their new vantage point into the streets and Squares of the surrounding valleys. They were, however, still without their own mechanical means of transport, the possession of a car amongst the younger generation still being something of a rarity in those post-war years.

Towns and villages in the Rhymni Valley were now, of course, more or less on their own doorstep, and access to those in the valleys to the East generally easier and cheaper than before. But westwards, apart perhaps from the Rhondda, the Cynon and Merthyr valleys via Pontypridd, the situation was more difficult. But there were the obvious compensations: the Movement in the South-East now had an independent and firmly established HQ, and Bargoed with its regular train service, was a venue comparatively easy of access by members from Caerdydd and the southern towns.

During the next months, Caerffili, Merthyr, Aberdâr, Y Coed Duon (*Blackwood*), Tredegar, Abertyleri and Pont-y-pŵl were amongst the towns harangued and then plied with *The Welsh Republican* paper in the pubs at night.

★ ★ ★

By the late Autumn however, those portents hinted at above had changed into hard, indisputable reality — the General Election in October had brought the Tories, the flagship party of English imperial nationalism back into power.

'*The Great Betrayal*', ran the headline over the front page story of the December-January 1952 issue of *The Welsh Republican*, with the simple stark figures boxed alongside:

Wales — 5 Tories, 27 Labour
England — 270 Tories, 233 Labour,
followed by:

" *'Came the Dawn'*

" 'What's the good of Welsh independence?' they used to ask us Welsh Republicans as we went around speaking and selling papers. 'We've got a Welsh government, haven't we? . . . We've got Aneurin Bevan and Jim Griffiths in the Cabinet; we've got full employment, we've got nationalisation; we've got the Welfare State. What more could we want?'

"What more indeed?

"History has not been slow in supplying the answer.

"What good now all those 20,000 majorities from Wrexham to the Rhondda?

"What price full employment now?

"What of the Welfare State?

"*The Dream is Over* — Cheltenham Spa and Tunbridge Wells have spoken. Our brothers, the people of England have given the orders, and it is for us the people of Wales to obey."

A Story of Betrayal, indeed — or more appropriately perhaps, of self-betrayal — and one still running more than forty years later in the closing years of the 20th Century.

The editorial too, deals, inevitably, and powerfully with that same sad story.

In a trenchant piece on page 4 of the paper, Alfred Pocock, a fighting patriot if ever there was one, under a chapter headed 'Taking not Begging', says of " . . . those who today pay lip-service to 'Home Rule' for Wales and draw up petitions asking England to grant them the smallest measure of self-government. How can England 'grant' to Wales that which does not belong to England? 'Home Rule' is but a term for the government which is ours when we desire to take it up. Because of England misrule Wales is humming today with talk of freedom; soon that hum will become a roar, and if success is to be gained, taking not begging will be the means."

Under a heading '*Death Sentence of Celtic Patriot*' reference is made to the case of Andre Geoffroy, Breton patriot, father of four children and outstanding personality of the Breton Nationalist Movement since 1924, who was sentenced to death by a French military tribunal on 13th November 1951.

This matter was to engage the attention and involve the activities of the WRM over the following year and more, and will be given due mention in later pages.

In his 'Letter to Mr Jones' Caradog deals appropriately, inimitably, with the comic-opera situation staged by the new Tory government in the appointment of lawyer Sir David Maxwell Fyfe (later, inevitably, known as Dai Bananas) to Minister for Welsh Affairs as a bit-part played in conjunction with his main rôle as English Home Secretary.

And in the end corner of the paper the Editor has made sure there is space for:

"*Na choelier Sais! Tri pheth nid oes daw arnynt: clep y felin, bwmbwr y môr, a chelwydd Sais (O lyfr Trioedd Beirdd Ynys Brydain, casgliad 1650).*"

* * *

Early in the Spring of 1952 Maxwell Fyfe announced in the wake of the Official Inquiry into the Tywi Valley afforestation plans that the Forestry Commission would not be given the necessary authority to proceed with the scheme. The announcement brought to an end the period of anxiety and stress suffered for so long, so cruelly and unnecessarily by the families of Maes Meddygon, Gallt y Berau, Troedyrhiw and the forty and more other farms concerned. Representatives of the WRM had taken an active part in the campaign to save the farms, and had made their presence and opinions strongly felt at the official Inquiry itself. But also, as Harri Webb put it in the April-May 1952 *Gweriniaethwr*: "What did the trick in Tywi? Pretty Speeches? Or the crudely daubed slogans on the walls of Llandovery calling on Rebecca to ride again, as she did a century ago, to rid the land of oppression?"

And, as he asked again concerning a decision made at about the same time to cancel War office plans to move into the Llŷn Peninsula: "What has saved the Llŷn smallholders for a space? Greasy Tory benevolence? Or the memory of Saunders Lewis' act of incendiary defiance in 1936 and the knowledge that any aggresion there would be a challenge that the manhood of re-arising Wales would meet in no uncertain manner?"

The fact that the Welsh Republicans were rapidly getting under the skin of the enemies of Wales in government was well and truly in evidence when David Llewellyn, Tory MP for Cardiff North, held aloft a copy of *The Welsh Republican* in the House of Commons, Westminster, to ask at a high pitch of indignation whether authority could not be brought to bear to "suppress the publication of this dangerous and subversive paper?" He seems to have read out an appropriate extract from the paper to try to reinforce his indignant call for some course of official action to bring that about. (But the painting of slogans on the wall of his house, St Quintins, at Llanfleiddan when he was entertaining there a Minister of the government, First Lord of the Admiralty,

J.P.L. Thomas, was perhaps not unconnected with this outburst.)

The organ of the Welsh Republican Movement had, however, another five good years of vigorous life to run, and if any additional steps were taken at that time to placate the fury of that renegade Welshman and his like, they must have been taken behind the overt political scene — such steps as we in the Republican Movement had very good reason, of course, to know were already in practice upon us.

As yet, we had not been troubled at the Bargoed address by visits from the police. But the following months were to see a change in the situation in that respect, with visits from Inspector Glyn Mathews of the Ystrad Mynach police HQ, and his gallant Sergeant in support, coming to darken the doorway of No. 104, Heol Gilfach on certain investigatory occasions. And on each of those occasions, as a strict rule of our household, they were never, even in the bleakest valley weather, invited to step up from the pavement into the comparative shelter of the doorway. Police actuated by unpatriotic political motives were then, as now, the least welcome visitors of all.

This was the time of the war in Korea when the threat of 'Z' and kindred army reserve call-up loomed to drag Welshmen back to war and the service of England's fading overseas empire. An article under the heading 'Z Reserve Injustice' in the April-May issue of the paper which was strongly critical of recent military actions in Egypt and Malaya had drawn considerable attention. "A few weeks ago in Ismailia, Egypt," it said, "the English army committed massacre. Fifty Egyptian military police, armed with rifles, were shot to pieces in their barracks at point-blank range by heavy tank guns. Of all the atrocities marked against England, it would be hard to find the equal of this in its methodical Teutonic deliberation." (The present writer remembers well the contemptuous, bullying behaviour of many amongst the occupying forces towards the native Egyptians during the war years, an attitude of gross imperialist intolerance which had obviously persisted into post-war years.) And a few sentences further on there is this:

> It is certain, however, that English army methods are no less thorough in Malaya than in Egypt. Via the French press there is recent news that six large Malayan villages have been obliterated for suspicion of harbouring guerrillas . . . They make a desert — and they call it peace . . . We believe that all young Welshmen of self-respect are with us in despising such deeds and their perpetrators . . . But do we as we stand under the shadow of English conscription or reserve re-call realize that call-up means that not only are we expected to turn a blind eye to such acts, but we are called up to commit them? . . . It is our responsibility as Welshmen to take every step available to make a dead letter of the English Services training organization so far as it

affects Wales and Welshmen."

Perhaps it was such an item as this that raised the blood-pressure of David Llewellyn M.P. to bursting point — and fairly certainly primed the authorities and their faithful political servants, the police, into readiness for appropriate action if and when decided upon.

Chapter 12

By the beginning of 1952 the case of Andre Geoffroy, Breton patriot under sentence of death in a French prison, was becoming a focus of attention for patriots in all the Celtic countries. The Welsh Republican Movement began to assume an important part in the urgent activities directed towards saving his life by bringing all possible pressure to bear on the French government.

From his early youth Geoffroy had been a member of the movement striving to restore Breton national independence after long centuries of domination and suppression by France. With the beginning of the retreat of the Germans from France and Brittany in 1944 the French found themselves free to exact vengeance against Bretons who during the war had taken advantage of the chance the war had given to try to re-establish their country's independence.

In 1944 Geoffroy was on the run from French retribution. He had already been sent to prison twice by the Germans. His wife, mother of four young children, was imprisoned by the French in his stead, in circumstances so harsh that she quickly fell ill of tuberculosis and was in danger of dying. Geoffroy surrendered in order to secure her release. He was sentenced to life imprisonment, which was then reduced to fifteen years hard labour.

In November 1951, during his eighth year of imprisonment, he was charged again, on the flimsiest of pretexts and the most doubtful and insubstantial evidence, of betraying two English spies to the Germans during the war. Redding and Abbot, the two spies, were imprisoned under comfortable conditions and both survived the war. It was alleged that they had given the Germans the naval code which made possible the escape of the German warships Prinz Eugen, Gneisenau and Scharnhorst down the English Channel by day. A French military tribunal, sitting with no jury, sentenced Geoffroy to death, despite the fact that the prosecutor had only asked for a sentence of 20 years. The records of his trial reek with the suggestion of rabid anti-Breton prejudice on the part of the tribunal judges, almost as if through such means they sought some sort of expiation for France's own feelings of wartime frailty and guilt.

In a letter to the Welsh Republican Movement dated 15th January 1952 from the prison of Fresnes, Geoffroy said that his appeal against the death sentence had been rejected. "The news," he wrote, "has dashed the hopes once again of my family, and it is the effect on them that troubles me most. Today I told my lawyer that I refuse to appeal for mercy to the President of the French Republic." He reasserted his innocence and asked only for justice. "I would prefer them to shoot me in my innocence than live under an unjust charge. Doesn't everybody have some consideration for his self-respect?" He said he had been greatly encouraged by many letters received from Wales and from Ireland, from Ulster, chiefly. *"C'est sans doute une question diplomatique"*, he thought was the reason why Dublin authorities seemed to have stopped letters from Éire, although in fact strong resolutions for his reprieve and release were eventually sent to the French President from Dublin, Cork, Galway, Tipperary, and Éire in general. The correspondence between the WRM and Geoffroy, his dedicated lawyer and others concerned in the case, was via the excellent idiomatic French of Huw Davies.

In Scotland a permanent Andre Geoffroy Committee was active and had asked the French President to receive a joint Celtic Deputation of Committees. In Wales, Dr D.J. Davies of Gilwern was preparing a case to present to the United Nations Committee of Human Rights, alleging that the sentence on Geoffroy was a flagrant use of the law to procure political ends, a political manoeuvre to keep him in prison for life, as, after his long years of imprisonment, he was to have been freed in the previous August under a general amnesty law.

Working in collaboration with Dr Ceinwen Thomas, Gilwern, the Welsh Republican Movement had drawn up a substantial memorandum of the facts of the case, and this was widely distributed in Britain and overseas.

The sentence on Geoffroy obtained publicity in the USA as an obvious breach of the Declaration of the Committee of the United Nations on Human Rights. Tom Williams, a member of the Council of the WRM, became Secretary of the Andre Geoffroy Welsh Committee, which obtained several thousands of signatures, including those of MPs and Church dignitaries, to a trilingual petition of appeal addressed to M. Auriol, the President of the French Republic.

Then news was received that two German prisoners kept in the same cell as Geoffroy had been taken out and summarily shot. This emphasized the need for more direct action by those fighting to save him from sharing their fate. Accordingly, Davies and Bere went to see the professional French Consul, M. Langlois, at his office, 103, The Exchange, Mount Stuart Square, Caerdydd. They felt confidently able to say after leaving his presence, that they had left him a very shaken, if not frightened, man near to the point perhaps of calling for help to free him of his visitors, and certainly with the message of fierce Celtic concern for Geoffroy very firmly impressed upon him; which undoubtedly was duly conveyed to Paris.

In April 1952 there came a further little opportunity for a gesture of concern over the fate of Andre Geoffroy. A visit was to be made on the 9th of the month to the Mayor and other institutions in Caerdydd by a party of four French journalists. They were to travel into the City via Bute Street after coming ashore in the Docks.

" . . . that you on the 9th day of April instant, at the City aforesaid, did unlawfully deface a wall at Bute Street by painting thereon without the permission of the owner," ran the wording of the summons served on Bere at the Bargoed address on the 25th of that month. This was probably the first doorway encounter in Bargoed with police faces that were to become more familiar to the resident Republicans there over the next year or two.

At the hearing of the summons at the Stipendiary Magistrate's Court, Caerdydd in the morning of 21st May it was related how Constable Peter Williams had come across the defendant in the middle of painting the words: 'FRANCE — LIBÉREZ ANDRE GEOFFROY' in large white letters on the long wall then bordering the east side of Bute Street. The fact that the defendant had returned to complete the unfinished work after the police-constable had left the scene was reported to the court.

Because of the defendant's persistent efforts to inform the court of the cruel injustice being perpetrated upon Andre Geoffroy and his impending fate and the urgent efforts being made in the Celtic countries and elsewhere on his behalf, the Stipendiary vented his frustration at the introduction of what he said he had to consider were political matters irrelevant to the case in hand, by deferring the case to the end of that day's long list.

Late in the afternoon the defendant was fined the sum of ten shillings, even in those days a quite nominal fine, and thereby leaving the impression that the case for Andre Geoffroy had perhaps after all touched a chord of sympathy somewhere in the legalistic mind of Mr Guy Sixsmith, Stipendiary Magistrate.

It was about this time that we came to hear of a young man, Jord Pinault by name, newly arrived in Cymru and claiming to be a Breton nationalist anxious to make contact with us in the WRM. When contact was made with him in Caerdydd we found him established in lodgings at the old Fitzhamon Embankment address of Webb and Bere.

For a few months he joined Republicans in certain of their activities such as paper selling and at open-air meetings. He was handled gingerly, however, and never taken into confidence of any serious import. How he was able to maintain himself was something of a mystery, and despite his seemingly genuine Breton patriotism and his eagerness to help in our activities, most of us could never free ourselves from feelings of suspicion about him.

He disappeared from our midst after a stay of a few months, almost as suddenly as he had arrived. Looking back from a distance of 40 years and more upon that little interval of acquaintance with Jord Pinault, all we are able to say is that if he was, still is, for all we know, a bona fide and patriotic citizen of Brittany we extend to him our belated regrets and apologies for the instinctive and inevitable suspicion we had of him.

In October 1952 Dr Ceinwen Thomas, Gilwern, who had been at the heart of the agitation in Cymru and elsewhere on Geoffroy's behalf, was appointed Secretary of the Celtic Congress, the organization whose aim was to promote co-operation and understanding between the Celtic nations. Although intensified efforts on behalf of Geoffroy had continued without pause throughout the year, on the 24th of December 1952 in a letter to *Y Faner* newspaper Dr Thomas was able to disclose the following facts: Andre Geoffroy had recently been moved from the Fresnes prison to the notorious La Santé, a place which had the severest prison regime in France. His feet and hands were now fettered throughout day and night. In Fresnes his feet had been chained day and night, but during the night his hands were freed. But in La Santé he remained chained even during the brief half hour a week he was allowed a visitor, when one warder stood behind the prisoner, and another behind the visitor; visiting time in Fresnes had been two hours a week. Now in La Santé his hand fetters were so short that they kept his hands crossed one upon the other all the time.

Pencil and paper were not allowed to him in his cell. His books were taken from him immediately he had read them. The prison was very cold, the food very poor. In appealing for all those fighting for Geoffroy to redouble their efforts, Dr Thomas gave the prison address to where letters might be sent to him. Who would believe that there could be such barbaric treatment of a prisoner in a country of Western Europe at this time, and in, of all countries, France? she asks. The obvious reason, she suggests, is that he is a defiant patriot of a country under the domination of France.

Chapter 13

The editorial of the June-July 1952 issue of *The Welsh Republican — Y Gweriniaethwr*, the subject of which is the Trade Unions in Wales, reads as though it might have been writen for the last decade of this century. It seems even more appropriate to this present day than to the day it was written. It was as if Huw Davies, in his last editorial before handing over his editorial pen into the hands of his successor, spoke in prophetic understanding:

"The Trade Unions in Wales have a proud history. From the struggles of past generations organizations of great strength have been built up. Welsh organized Labour now has power and responsibilities which can make for a still prouder future. The continued progress of the Welsh Nation depends to a considerable extent on the character of the leadership given by the Welsh Labour Movement.

"The people of our industrial valleys and communities, in North and South, have never been afraid of militant opposition to injustice and exploitation. Dire povery and suffering were spurs to workers' organization. Defence of the family and the fight for raised living standards became great moral issues in our industrial areas. Resort to physical force, and more recently to syndicalist action, has often marked the growth of the Welsh Labour Movement. Perhaps because of this the high purpose of the Movement has been sometimes overlooked, alike by Nonconformists, Liberal Nationalists of the Cymru Fydd period, and comfortable patriots of this generation. But the main course of Welsh democratic development in face of industrialisation has been through the conflicts and strikes in the mines, mills and quarries of our country. With the added political experience of the last decades, organised Welsh Labour has become a vital factor in the achievement of Welsh Independence.

"At present, however, the Welsh Trade Unions are not providing enough of the leadership which we should expect. Over-riding English influence and control has resulted from the mergers with English Unions and the continued attachment to the English Trades

Union Congress. Whilst there were strong arguments for merging with the English Unions in view of the political subordination of Wales to England, it is now clear that much has been lost. Initiative is stifled. Action in sympathy with Welsh aspirations is hampered. Faced with English Conservative government contrary to the will of the majority of the Welsh People, the Welsh Trade Unions remain acquiescent in the supine attitude of the English T.U.C. dignitaries.

"It would be idle to blame the Welsh Trade Unionists for this situation. The loss of identity of the Welsh Unions is but one more example of the weaknesses of being without national sovereignty. But now is the time for constructive leadership in the Welsh Labour Movement. Independence of action must be regained. This does not preclude co-operation with English, Scottish and Irish organizations. The Scottish Trade Union Congress might serve as an example to the Welsh Unions. They would be more effective if similarly organized.

"The real aims of Welsh Labour must be recognized. They are related to the maintenance of employment, the development of the social services and education, the provision of housing and communal amenities, the prevention of labour transference and military and industrial conscription for English ends. These aims are essentially the aims of the Welsh Republican Movement. To achieve National Independence is manifestly the next objective of Welsh Labour if this social progress is to be ensured. The opportunities of the Welsh Unions are thus apparent. All the methods of Union organization, and industrial and political agitation can be adopted to serve the interests of our People. So the reaction, injustice and misdirection of resources typical of English government of Wales will be ended."

The 'Guilty Man' in this issue was none other than Captain Roderick Bowen, QC, MA, LlB, MP — for reasons 'Spy' seemed to think more than adequate.

An informative article by Sean Tozer of the Irish Anti-Partition Association on 'Lessons from Norway and Sweden' supplies a valuable potted history of the Scandinavian nations and offers a lesson that cries out to be taken to heart by the subject nations of Britain:

> "The union between Denmark, Sweden and Norway under the Danish Crown, which took place in 1389 was (like the British 'union') supposed to be based on 'equal partnership'. In 1521 the Swedes had begun to feel that the Danes were 'having everything their own way', and they organized a successful rebellion . . . The Norwegians did not revolt. They remained united with Denmark against their wishes until 1814. In that year Denmark suffered a military defeat in alliance

with Napoleon, and by the terms of the peace treaty Norway was handed over into union with Sweden. By this union Norway became a junior partner to Sweden, instead of, as previously, to Denmark. In 1905 the Norwegian people had become tired of being used as pawns in the game of power politics. Their parliament openly defied the authority of Sweden. For a time it looked as if there would be a war. A plebiscite of the Norwegian people had voted almost unanimously for independence; and the Swedish Parliament accepted the verdict. We in Ireland had a different experience after the election in 1918. The Sinn Fein victory was followed by a visit from the Black & Tans . . . Sweden and Norway have shown us how to achieve independence from a dominant neighbour. In like manner the three Celtic races can assert their independence of the English, from whom they differ fundamentally in race, temperament and language. We in Ireland look forward to the triumph of the Welsh Republican Movement as our struggle is against the same enemy."

On another page Dr Ceinwen Thomas ends her impressive piece headed 'Welsh Labour Must Give Lead' with the following plea:

"In England all the political parties forget party differences when their country is in danger, and work unitedly until the danger is over. We call on patriotic Welsh people to do likewise, and the Labour Party in Wales must give a lead in this matter. It must embark on a new course as the Labour Party of Wales, with the emphasis on the word 'Wales', until our country is made free and independent. Let all true Welsh people in the Labour ranks bring their party into the fight for Welsh freedom."

★ ★ ★

Huw Davies' aptitude for politics and his selfless devotion to the activities in which it involved him were nevertheless by no means the be-all and end-all of life for him. From his early youth he had been an accomplished all-round sportsman. So accomplished, in fact, that he had played for the Glamorgan Seconds County Cricket team. In the rugby season he played for one of the Glamorgan Wanderers' teams. There were occasions, therefore, on Saturday usually, when even *his* political dedication had to make way for sport.

Midway through a naval officer's training course at Dartmouth at the end of the war, Huw had withdrawn from the course, telling the commanding officer there, to that man's amazement and consternation, that as a Welsh Nationalist he could no longer continue with the course. But if by taking that decisive step Huw Davies had very likely put himself beyond the reach of any designs on him the armed forces might have had for recall to service, Cliff Bere on the other hand (he had served for nearly six years in the armed forces, mainly in North Africa), seemed to have remained a prime target for recall. This was the time of the Anglo-American war in Korea. After demobilization in 1946, it seems that Bere had been placed, without any suggestion of a 'by-your-leave', on the 'Z' Reserve military recall roll. He had already written more than once in *The Welsh Republican* on the infamy of this practice so far as it would affect, in particular, Welsh ex-servicemen. And now, lo and behold! — as if fickle fate were playing for a little laugh — or possibly the military themselves were in vengeful mood — he received call-up papers under 'Z' Reserve.

First had come a notice (dated 25th February 1952) requesting him to report for medical examination at a Caerdydd location.

It was ignored.

Came a second notice, dated 8th March.

Also ignored.

Then quickly (11th March) came the follow up, *commanding*:

" 1. You are hereby called up for training . . .
2. You will present yourself to Aberporth, Cards. on 13th April 1952 . . .
5. You are warned, etc . . .
9. You will also note and comply with, etc . . .
10. You will acknowledge receipt of this notice by signing the attached . . . "

This 'command' was duly returned to sender at Reading, England with a couple of WRM printed adhesive labels attached — 'No more Blood for England' and 'Z Reserve — Does dim Z yn y Gymraeg'.

On the 21st of April came a visit to the door of 104, Heol Gilfach by Police Inspector Glyn Mathews of Ystrad Mynach, another close contact view of a face that was to become more than a little familiar in that doorway. "Are you a Z reservist?" the Inspector asked Bere. "Yes, it seems I am," he was told. Asked if he had received a notice to report for training, Bere said: "Yes, I have." Asked further if he had applied for exemption, Bere replied: "No, and I don't intend to," adding: "The English army has no authority over me as a Welshman."

A summons, The Queen against Bere, dated 24th June 1952, duly arrived, served by the hand of Inspector Mathews himself and accompanied by an order over the personal signature of the Director of Public Prosecutions requiring the production at the hearing of the summons, on the 18th of the next month, of the call-up notice and another earlier communication from the Ministry of Labour and National Service. (It would seem that liaison between the army authorities and the DPP had not been of the highest order of efficiency.)

At the hearing in Bargoed Police Court on the 18th of July Bere told the court he belonged to the Welsh Republican Movement, one of whose aims was to drive English khaki out of Wales. "There are names like Ismailia," he said, "which stick in one's throat and make one sick. If you think you can coerce me into the English army again under those conditions, you are misled. England has no rightful claim over Welshmen. England's army is her own concern. Wales would have her own army, but it would be a Welsh army based on her own soil, and its only purpose would be to defend its own soil. There is resistance in Wales against English conscription. The time is coming to an end when England would have Welshmen at her service. I call on Welshmen of self-respect to take the same stand as I am taking. It is time to call a halt to the exploitation of the Welsh people." His words drew shouts of approval from several young men in the courtroom.

Mr W.E.J. McDonnell, London, prosecuted for the Director of Public Prosecutions on information laid by Superintendent William Folland. The Chairman of the magistrates on the Bench was Mr A.S. Williams, who had presided over the Caerffili court in August 1950 when Bere and Evans had been fined for burning the imperial banner on the tower of Castell Caerffili.

The defendant had told his wife, now mother of two young children, that he expected on this occasion to be sentenced to a term of imprisonment, the maximum penalty to which he was liable being a fine of £50 together with a month in prison. But the Chairman, who during the proceedings had asserted his own patriotism as a Welshman, could possibly have been making something of a gesture towards substantiating that claim of his when he imposed the lesser penalty of a £20 fine and £4-4-0 costs — with 14 days in which to pay.

The amount was paid out of the WRM courts fund contributed to by many supporters; the renewed appeal launched in July 1952 over the name of Tom Williams had brought in a response as generous as that to the earlier appeal of a year or so before.

A later generation of young patriots, however, have often elected to go to prison rather than pay fines inflicted, and our regard for them is all the greater for that.

★ ★ ★

From the August-September 1952 issue, *The Welsh Republican* was in the hands of a new Editor, Ifor Huws Wilks, as a representative of the northern Republicans. He had graduated with first-class honours at Bangor University College, and although now engaged on a two year period of research study at Oxford University had been more than willing to take on the burden of the editorship. A letter from him dated 15th May 1951 from Bangor is indicative of his wholehearted commitment to the cause of Cymru via the Welsh Republican Movement:

> "Now that the time (of exams) is so near I'm able to think beyond it once again — to renewing active contact with MGC. Though I'm not so sure just how bright the prospect is - as I think I told you, I have a place in Oxford to do research; but I just cannot decide whether to take it. I hate the thought of leaving Wales for two years — though on the other hand after that two years I shall be able with luck to get a post either in one of the Welsh University Colleges, or in Coleg Harlech or some other such establishment. But I can hardly bear to think of uprooting myself from Bangor — I have lived in England so long, and have craved to be back in Wales, that it seems ridiculous to leave again. Ah well, I'll let you know within a few weeks what I'll be doing.
>
> "Will John Legonna still be in Oxford next year? Is he working on the potential periodical still? Are there any other contacts in Oxford? Would there be anything useful I could do there? — not likely, is it!"

It is a tribute to the youthful enthusiasm of Ifor Wilks, even more so under the circumstances in which he found himself in that summer of 1952, that he was prepared to take on himself a task for which Huw Davies had set so high a standard. The correspondence that flowed between Wilks and Bargoed leading up to the publication of that August-September issue, the first for which he was to be responsible, was an almost daily succession of requests for advice and suggestions about contents and printing procedures, which showed his concern to ensure that the paper should continue to strike the same veins of effectiveness as before.

In the event, that first issue under his editorship was something of a disappointment — to Wilks himself in particular, although his editorial was probably its best feature:

> "We present this first number of a new volume on rising tides of optimism and of anger," he said. "Our optimism is surely well justified! For, as a writer in this issue points out, the strength of Wales lies in its working classes. Everywhere in Wales, despite centuries of English domination, the working classes hold firm to their nationality. From Holyhead to Cardiff, and from Monmouthshire to the Irish Sea, irrespective of language or religion, the common people are still swift to proclaim themselves Welsh, still proud of their own distinctive heritage. *Yet, their nationalism manifests itself in no backward-looking romanticism, but in a drive to social justice, which makes the Welsh one of the most progressive people in the whole of Western Europe, and one of the least totalitarian.* Yet our opinion does not rest here alone. A great people may be impoverished through want and

privation; but here in Wales we are rich in natural resources, *with room still for immense industrial and agricultural undertakings*. By contemporary standards, we are still both under-capitalised and under- populated. In all this there is certainly just cause for optimism . . . Yet if our optimism is justified, so too is our anger."

After cataloguing a few of those just causes for anger, he ended:

"What then is the answer to all this? . . . There is but one answer. Only within the framework of an independent Welsh State can the rich, under-developed natural resources of Wales be exploited in the interests of the Welsh people. And only within such a Welsh State can the demand for social justice and equality find full expression. It is to fight for such an independent State that the Welsh Republican Movement has committed itself."

A piece by Cliff Bere, 'Welsh Citizens, not English Subjects', and one on 'The English Monarchy — Symbol of Welsh Subjection', by Harri Webb, and a back page assault (by the Editor himself) on the hypocrisy of the pretension of *The Western Mail* of those days in offering itself as the 'National Daily of Wales', make up the greater part of the remainder of the issue, together with a quite extensive correspondence column, including a letter from Irishman Sean MacStíobáin. There is a short but pertinent piece by Gwynfor Thomas, Nantgarw, on the front page, and a brief report of the Z Reserve case at Bargoed court. 'Mr Jones' had to make do with a very abbreviated 'Letter from Caradog', and Spy's 'Guilty Man' was held over, for this issue, at least.

Perhaps the reason for the Editor's disappointment with this his first issue of the paper was not so much to do with the content in itself, but in the printing errors in the 'streaming' of columns at the beginning of articles, for instance, and the unaccountable omission of sub-headings over smaller items, not to mention a glaring printing gaffe in the front-page title of the paper. Not all of these could be put down to editorial inexperience.

However, the next issue of the paper was in almost all respects 'back on the rails' and running full-steam ahead. But it was in the next issue after that again, for December 52 - January 53, by now flaunting its name in proud red type, that Ifor Wilks came to full flower as an editor. And to that issue and its 'explosive' contents, full reference will be made in due chronological order.

★ ★ ★

As to the Bookshop and Library business, however, things were not going well. After its opening on 17th September 1951 it had attracted a reasonable amount of business despite its situation a little distance away from the main shopping area of the town. An encouraging boost in trade over the Christmas period had given hope that it could at least provide a subsistence income for Harri Webb who was in charge of it. He had organized an efficient system for the library side of the business, and this, in particular, had continued to flourish in a modest way during the early months of 1952. But with the approach of summer, business, even in the library section, diminished to such an extent that it became not worthwhile to keep it open, and on the 7th of June 1952 Siop Lyfrau a Llyfrgell Bargoed came to the end of its all too brief venture into the business life of that town.

Within a very short time, as a matter of economic necessity, Harri Webb had obtained a post as librarian in Cheltenham. He kept in very close touch with Bargoed by correspondence and was still able to play an essential part in the affairs of the Movement. He visited Bargoed regularly from his temporary exile and was often available to take part in weekend meetings continuing to be held on the streets of valley towns. Within a year or so he was able to return from England to take up a library post in Dowlais.

But in retrospect, they were happy enough days. Behind the scenes, Eluned Rhys Bere and her two little sons, Iwan and Gareth, were very busy. Huw Davies continued in employment as export executive with Cory Bros., Caerdydd, and during the Spring Cliff Bere had been employed in the area of Caerdydd Docks too, by the Camrex Paint Company. Later in the year he had taken a job in Ystradmynach with one of the Julian Hodge concerns.

One of the disadvantages of having Harri Webb tied to the shop on Saturdays had been that Davies and Bere were deprived of his services on some of their speaking trips. But now, on the frequent occasions when he was able to return for a weekend, and thus formidably reinforced, they were able to return with him to renew acquaintance with many a listener at some of their favourite venues. A meeting on Saturday, 23rd August at the town Square in Bryn-mawr on one of these occasions stands out in the memory.

A little incident at about this time fairly certainly shows that police surveillance of the Republicans was in process of development. A well-known Wales-based representative of the London *Daily Mirror* newspaper, accompanied by cameraman, called at No. 104, Heol Gilfach. His assignment, he said, was to obtain photographs of prominent members of the WRM to illustrate a story his paper was intending to run concerning the Movement. He gave a detailed description of how the story would be presented. Republican members in Swansea, he said, had already allowed their photographs to be taken for the project.

He and the cameraman were shown the door in Bargoed, with the threat of a boot to speed their exit. There had been more than one occasion in the past when attempted camera shots by newspaper men in Caerdydd on behalf of, it was presumed, the police had been anticipated and, hopefully, frustrated.

It was never confirmed that Abertawe members, if they *had* been visited, had in fact fallen for the bait. As expected, nothing appeared in *The Daily Mirror* in relation to the incident.

★ ★ ★

Later on in the Autumn of 1952, 104, Heol Gilfach saw much more welcome visitors, amongst them, Rhydwyn Pughe of Bryncrug, Meirion, who arrived again on his big motor-bike to stay for a night or two. A week or two later came Wilks for a short sojourn amongst the people of the Valleys about whose lives and history he was to speak and write along the years in learned and graphic style.

On a Saturday, 11th October, Webb, Davies and Wilks went across to Merthyr Tudful where, speaking on the scene of older Welsh uprisings, they had the main street of the town echoing again with their call for Wales to face the need for a new and final rebellion. A powerful attack by Wilks on the shameful un-Welsh attitudes and actions of David Llewellyn, MP for Cardiff North, was a notable feature of the occasion.

In the meantime, however, on Sunday, 5th October, the Welsh Republican Movement had joined forces with Welsh, Scottish and Irish nationalists at a great rally in Trafalgar Square, London, under the banners of the Celtic Alliance, led there from Hyde Park by massed Scots and Irish pipers. From the plinth of the Nelson Column the renowned Wendy Wood spoke for Scotland, Meredydd Edwards for Plaid Cymru, and, between two Irish orations, Harri Webb for Mudiad Gweriniaethol Cymru spoke with the fiercest eloquence of all.

"You'll do it before us yet," Wendy Wood told a member of WRM a few weeks later after the event described in the following chapter.

Chapter 14

Early in the morning of Monday, 20th October 1952 the residents in 104, Heol Gilfach picked up the *Western Mail* from behind the front door to see the headline splashed across the front page telling of a big explosion in the early hours of the previous day at the Elan aqueduct which carried Birmingham's water supply from Wales. This was stirring news for the household. But before long Huw Davies left the house to walk to Gilfach Halt to catch his train. Not long after, Cliff Bere left to cycle down to his work at Glam-Mon Motors in Ystradmynach.

By the time they returned towards evening there was a police constable stationed at the edge of the wide pavement fronting the house and shop. He seemed to note their arrivals, but made no attempt to approach them. It seems he had been there since late morning. Life had gone on as usual in the house; there had been no callers there. A constable was stationed outside throughout that night and the next day. But no move was made to call at the house or question the comings and goings of those living there.

On Thursday morning the 23rd October Bere arrived at his place of work in Ystradmynach to be told that he would have to end his employment there that day. The new Claerwen dam was to be formally opened by the English queen in the afternoon of that very same day. The explosion had been on the great pipeline fifteen miles from the dam.

Bere decided not to challenge such a summary dismissal, and said that in that case he would leave at midday. No, you have to stay until the end of the day he was told — so emphatically indeed, that he half expected the police to be called in to ensure against his too premature departure. But leave by midday, he did.

He was back in Bargoed in about half an hour, to see, parked a few yards up from No. 104 a motor-car with two men inside, both of them apparently engrossed in reading their newspapers as per the time-honoured car-snooping code. His wife told him that they had not been there half an hour earlier. It did, indeed, seem that there could be some sort of liaison between police and place of work.

After lunch he took a walk to the Capel Arms a couple of hundred yards down the road. As he entered the pub he saw the police car following him down. Ten minutes or so later he left the pub and saw that the car was parked a few yards further up the road. As he crossed the road towards a street leading up past the Miners' Institute he saw one of the policemen leave the car. Bere went quickly up round the curve of the street and out of sight of the following man and entered the Institute building and up to the first floor from where he was able to look out on the street. He saw his would-be shadower hurry on past after hesitating a moment before the entrance to the building.

After waiting a minute or two for him to get far enough out of the way and hopefully out of sight, Bere left the building and crossed to a roadway leading up out of the town. He soon found that he had lost his shadower. For the next two or three hours he communed with the pleasant Autumn scenery in the countryside high above Bargoed.

By the end of the afternoon, that the official ceremony of appropriation of Claerwen water free and for nothing for the use of the English midlands had no doubt taken place without further incident, he was ready to assume, so there could be nothing to lose by releasing the searching police from their anxiety. And what an anxious few hours they'd had! he soon saw. Hurrying up a narrow path towards him as he approached the town was the very worried-looking gone-astray shadower, who immediately fell in behind his quarry and kept no more than a close pace behind him for the rest of the way back to 104, Heol Gilfach. Not a word was exchanged between this strange duo. Bere went into the house and his shadow disappeared — perhaps to continue searching — this time for his companion in the car.

The Republican household soon discovered that they had been under even closer surveillance than indicated by the above incidents. They found out that the front bedroom of the house next door had been occupied by the police to help keep them under observation. And the small window high in the gable end of the little chapel overlooking the rear of their premises was also almost certainly made use of for that purpose. The probability of which brought a rueful smile or two later to the faces of those who had on occasions exited from No. 104 via the back window in the hope of thereby avoiding detection.

★ ★ ★

"! EXPLOSION! — As the English Press saw it" ran a column headline in the next issue of *The Welsh Republican*, quoting:

"*Daily Graphic*, October 20th — Police stood guard last night on the Fron Aqueduct, in Radnorshire, in mid-Wales, after an explosion early in the day under one of its 26 arches. The aqueduct carries Birmingham's water supply over the river Ithon from the Elan Valley reservoir . . . The Fron aqueduct is 16 miles from the new Claerwen valley dam, which the Queen is to open on Thursday, and it was thought the explosion might be connected with the Royal visit. The explosive was placed in the wall of the aqueduct apparently to destroy the pipeline which carries millions of gallons of water to the Birmingham area. The blast heard up to two miles away, caused an 8 ft crater in the arch."

"*Daily Herald* October 21st — A gelignite charge detonated by an alarm clock delay device exploded under one of the arches of the 36ft high viaduct . . . Welsh Nationalists here have been the first to condemn the outrage, but they and the police incline to the theory that the bomb may have been planted by members of the extremist Welsh Republican Party, which holds any weapon fair in the fight for home rule.

Only determined men with local knowledge could have planned the operation. The explosive charge, which weighed several pounds, had to be carried in pitch darkness through pouring rain, down a boggy hillside and through a wood, every yard of the way riddled with knee-deep potholes.

"*Daily Herald*, October 23rd — A half-ton boulder of granite crashed shortly before midnight from a Welsh mountainside near the new Claerwen dam at Rhayader, on the road along which the Queen and the Duke of Edinburgh will drive today on their way to open the dam. Police in a patrol car on security duties, instituted following Sunday's bomb outrage 15 miles away, found the boulder and debris partly blocking the road at a spot known as Devil's Leap. They radioed the news to Security headquarters, which controls the movement of 500 police and 200 soldiers who have been drafted into the area."

"*London Evening News*, October 23rd — Special Branch men from Scotland Yard and scores of detectives from three counties swept along the narrow mountain road here today in a dawn check on the 20-mile Royal route to Claerwen Dam. It was the climax of one of the biggest Royal Security Plans launched by the police. By the time the Queen and the Duke of Edinburgh leave here tonight after opening the dam, more than 1000 plain clothes and uniformed men will have been engaged in the hunt for the saboteurs who five days ago attempted to blow up the pipeline taking water to Birmingham.

"Early today a Home Office explosive expert gave his report on the explosion which rocked the valley on Sunday. It did not, I understand, allay the fears of police chiefs that the sabotage attempt was the work of determined men. Fresh orders went out to the 500 policemen who will line the Royal route to arrest anyone acting suspiciously."

* * *

On 25th October, the Saturday after the explosion, Huw Davies and Cliff Bere shared a memorable experience. They had taken the bus from Bargoed to Y Coed Duon (*Blackwood*) in the neighbouring valley, carrying with them a full supply of the October-November issue of *The Welsh Republican*. In the early evening they spoke on the street to an appreciative gathering and enjoyed an encouraging sale of the paper. Later on, keeping an eye on the bus departure time, they took the paper into The Rock Inn in Tredegar Road. The crowded pub was a hubbub of Saturday night talk. But as soon as they had entered the door, red-titled Republican paper displayed, there fell on the room a silence that stays in the memory still.

Then those mining men found their voices again.

"Don't forget us next time — we'll be with you!" . . . "We'll do the job for you! — let us know when" . . . It was almost an embarrassment of enthusiasm around the two Republicans as they went from table to table with papers, shaking outstretched hands, selling, fumbling for small change that was almost always refused. "Next time, we'd like to be with you! Yes, boys — don't forget! Don't forget!" were the words and sentiments ringing in their ears as they went out of the pub door, papers all gone, pockets heavy with coin.

Yes — to some extent it could have been the beer talking, the happy two had to acknowledge to themselves on the journey home. However — *in vino veritas* — there was more than a grain of comfort for them in that thought.

But in rather unhappy contrast to the sentiments voiced so enthusiastically by the miners of Y Coed Duon and many, many others, the Fron aqueduct explosion drew down upon the heads of whoever had been responsible for it only harsh criticism and public condemnation by some well-known nationalists who, it is certainly our opinion, ought to have made wiser judgment. There was a regrettable instance of this attitude at a nationalist rally in Sir Fôn a few days after the incident, when responsibility and condemnation for it was directly levelled at the Republicans. It is an attitude which is still echoing in the nationalist politics of today. Whether or not it is the right one will be decided eventually by the realities of the situation facing Cymru in the fight for her future.

* * *

The editorship of the *Welsh Republican — Y Gweriniaethwr* rose most ably to the occasion with its coverage of the Fron aqueduct explosion in the following issue, December-January, of the paper. As already noted, there were extensive quotes of the publicity given to the incident by the English press. Wilks' editorial itself richly deserves its fair share of quotation. It begins:

> "A 'warm' welcome indeed was afforded the English queen on her recent visit to mid-Wales, attempts being made to blow up the Fron aqueduct and, apparently, to block the Elan Valley road. When it became evident that determined Welshmen had protested against the wholesale English exploitation of Welsh resources, not in words alone, but in deeds, the English authorities were sent into a panic for the safety of their queen. Emergency security measures were rushed into effect, which certainly testified to the salutary terror created in English hearts by this display of Welsh striking power.
>
> "For several decades Welsh interests have been defended at most by resolutions, never by resolution. The burning of the Penyberth aerodrome in 1936 by three Welsh Nationalists, who promptly gave themselves up to the police, indeed did something to break the sterility of the inter-war years. But in perspective, this action appears more as a symbolic gesture of personal martyrdom than as a declaration of war. Not so the recent attack on the Birmingham pipeline — for the men who planted the bomb under the aqueduct in Radnorshire did not surrender to the police, but faded quietly away into a background of ordinary Welsh homes, where doubtless they survive, prepared to strike again, and again, and again, until the whole fabric of the centuries-old English rule in Wales lies utterly and finally shattered. It may be that in the events of October 19th, 1952, Wales has witnessed the first blow struck by the first armed Welsh Resistance Movement of the 20th century." . . .

It concludes:

> "Exploitation, and the denial of the rights of any nation to rule its own affairs, breeds, and always has and always will breed, resistance to the exploiting power. It is, Welshmen have learnt, noble and praiseworthy to take up arms for the freedom of self-government as guaranteed by the signatories of the United Nations Atlantic Charter. *It would be strange indeed were not many Welshmen to realize that it may be equally noble and praiseworthy to fight for that very same freedom when it is denied to their own nation, Wales.*
>
> "That, at least, appears to be the lesson of October 19th. If so, then LET ENGLAND BEWARE!"

An item on the front page reports an incident at Ffair Borth (*Menai Bridge Fair*) a few days after the Fron aqueduct explosion: " . . . when a group of young Welshmen who openly expressed their approval of the attack on the pipeline were violently assaulted by the police. One was struck across the mouth by a police Inspector, and a second man kicked. Only the hostile attitude of the crowd towards the police prevented further of these assaults in the name of English Law and Order."

Another timely piece is provided by a member of the now 'notorious' Republican Movement. Under the heading 'We will not only speak for Wales . . . We will act on her behalf', it explains:

"The state has been described as the skeleton of the Nation. There is no need to look farther than Wales today to realize how apt this definition is. The Welsh nation without self-government is the body and brains without the bones — an entity without power to move for itself or to fulfil its aims and aspirations. The nation without statehood, without sovereign executive power, is an inert and stagnating society.

"The Welsh Republican Movement exists to establish the statehood of Wales, and to make her once again a complete and vital entity amongst the nations of the world. Which means that the duties and tasks of Welsh statehood, i.e., the prosecution and the defence of our nation's interests, lie for the present on the shoulders of the young men and women of the Welsh Republican Movement alone. *In the absence of Wales' own government, the Welsh Republican Movement will not only speak for Wales — it will also act on her behalf.*

"It is a proud duty for Welsh Republicans. It is also a dangerous duty. For English domination and exploitation of our country is carried on through the instrumentality of English Law, with all the resources of the English State available to enforce it.

"*But as we take our stand for Wales against the power of the English State our inspiration is the knowledge of the responsibility we bear, and our conviction is that in the decisive hour we shall have at our sides the incomparable and united poeple of the Welsh nation.*"

But the excellence of this issue of the paper is by no means confined to coverage of the Elan Valley incident. Under the heading 'The Rebecca Revolt — an Armed Welsh Insurrection', it contains an important introductory article by Ifor Huws Wilks to a subsequent series of studies by him in *The Welsh Republican* on the history of Welsh rebellion against English rule in the 19th century. (In later years Ifor Wilks was to publish a classic work on this theme, 'South Wales and the Rising of 1839'.)

There is also in this issue of the paper the second of what was to become the celebrated series of 'potted histories' of Wales by Harri Webb — 'Glorious

Episodes from our Past or . . . What they don't allow to be taught in Welsh Schools'. This episode is about the Merthyr Rising of 1831, when " . . . Dick Penderyn was captured, handed over to 'justice' and was hanged in Cardiff gaol."

And on another brief, sad note this issue of the paper ends:

"OBITUARY — 14th September 1952, Tecwyn Lloyd Owen, Tywyn, Merioneth. Formerly an Organizer for Plaid Cymru, Tecwyn Owen joined the Welsh Republican Movement shortly before his untimely death at the age of 25. His loss could ill be afforded."

* * *

In contrast to the Bookshop and Library, however, the business of *The Welsh Republican* paper was flourishing. The number of subscribers to the paper had been steadily increasing throughout 1951/2, and by the beginning of 1953 it was approaching 300. The subscription list covered a wide range of personalities, from the revolutionary and merely radical, to the most constitutionalist and conservative-minded of public and political figures, more than a few of them from overseas countries. The Consulat de France, 103, The Exchange, Caerdydd was now numbered amongst the paid-up subscribers. The work of despatching the paper by post was a chore which kept the inhabitants of no. 104 busy for a day or two on the publication of each issue.

A long article in *Y Cymro* newspaper in December 1952 by David Raymond, a journalist of international repute, makes interesting reading:

"*O Dde Cymru, anfonodd darllenydd anhysbys (i'm goleuo, hyd y gwelaf i) gopi o'r 'Welsh Republican' — newyddiadur y Gweriniaethwyr Cymreig — sydd yn dymuno Senedd i Gymru — a llawer yn ychwaneg.*

"*Ond tra bod Lady Megan yn hyderu y cyrhaeddir y nod trwy gyfrwng cyfarfodydd cyhoeddus a phenderfyniadau, y mae'r Gweriniaethwyr yn argymell defnyddio ffyrdd llawer mwy chwyldroadol. Yn wir, os nad wyf yn dallgibio wrth ddarllen erthyglau eu papur, y maent yn apelio am rywbeth lled tebyg i Mau Mau Cymreig.*

"*Efallai bravado sy'n achosi iddynt fynnu mewn iaith glir a diamwys, mai gwladgarwyr Cymreig a achosodd y ffrwydrad a ddigwyddodd yng Nghlaerwen y Sul cyn ymweliad y Frenhines ym mis Hydref. Ond bravado neu beidio, y ffaith arwyddocâol yw nad oes swildod o gwbl yn enaid y 'Gweriniaethwr' wrth glodfori'r digwyddiad fel gweithred gyntaf Byddin Arfog gyntaf Cymru yn yr oes hon.*"

He goes on to say, after first quoting (in Welsh translation) from the editorial of *Y Gweriniaethwr* on the Fron aqueduct explosion:

"*Y mae Braw yn arf y mae'r mwyafrif yn ei chashau, yn enwedig cenedl mor llyweth â'r Cymry. Er hyn y mae modd cyfiawnhau brawychu fel ffordd o ennill delfryd. Y mae digon o enghreifftiau hanesyddol o oruchafiaeth y bwgan Ofn.*" . . .

"*Y gŵr addfwyna' fyw oedd yr Americanwr H.D. Thoreau, a fynnai yn anad neb y dylid defnyddio unrhyw foddion i ddarostwng gormesydd. Braenarodd y tir ar gyfer y Chwyldro Americanaidd a fwriodd oddi ar ysgwyddau'r wlad iau'r Brenin Seisnig Sior III.*

"*Rhyfedd yw meddwl fel y molir canlyniadau'r gwŷr sy'n defnyddio Braw fel arf rhyfel, er i'r gwŷr eu hunain gael eu condemnio yn foesol oherwydd eu gweithredoedd!*

"*Y mae Iwerddon yn un enghraifft o oruchafiaeth braw. Israel yn enghraifft arall. A all y rhai a gythruddwyd gan weithredoedd y Gwyddelod a'r Iddewon ddweud mewn difrif y buasent wedi ennill eu rhyddid onibae am y moddion brawychus a ddefnyddiasant?*

"*Neu i roddi enghraifft amserol, a fuasem wedi cytuno i ffurfio comisiwn i ystyried hen gwynion yr Affricanwyr yn Kenya, oni bai bod y Mau Mau, trwy gyfrwng eu gweithredoedd difrifol wedi ein deffro o drymgwsg difaterwch? Wrth gondemnio'r Mau Mau, gedwch inni hefyd ein condemnio ein hunain am inni oddef yr amgylchiadau y tyfodd y mudiad ynddynt.*"

* * *

The February-March 1953 *Welsh Republican* more than maintains the high standard of previous issues. Alongside the powerful case made on the front page for Welsh miners fighting the Tory government for a fair pay deal, there are two other items worthy of notice. A short excerpt from the one titled 'Wales must have Freedom', suffices to convoy its message and give due honour to the Councillor named in it:

> "Protesting against the slavishness and servility of a motion placed before Anglesey County Council expressing appreciation of the royal decision to include a Welsh emblem on the English coinage, Councillor O.T.L. Huws gave notice of a counter motion. 'Rather than support a resolution which savours of servility,' stated the Councillor, 'would it not be nobler, more dignified and worthy of our heritage, that the question of the union of Wales and England be reviewed, and that the infamous and tyrannous Act of 1536 be repealed and replaced by an Act that would be based on the recognition of a respect for absolute equality between the two nations,

their respective cultures, traditions and customs?' "

The other item, under the heading 'Money for African Leader in Kenya', records as follows:

"In accordance with the spirit of the Welsh Republican Manifesto, at a Republican meeting held in Cardiff recently it was decided that a sum of money should be donated by the Welsh Republican Movement towards the cost of the defence of Jomo Kenyatta, President of the Kenya Africa Union, as a token of admiration for the struggles of the people of Kenya against the vicious exploitation of their land and labour by England.

"The following reply was received from the Secretary of the Kenya Africa Union:

'Dear Sir,

We have received the sum of money, through Mr D.N. Pritt, donated by your organisation towards the defence of our National President, Mr Jomo Kenyatta. This gesture touches our hearts and I am asked by Mr Jomo Kenyatta personally and by other leaders now on trial to express their deep sense of gratitude for your gesture.

'Mr Pritt is putting up a very strong defence in this case and we admire his courage and determination to see that justice is done.
Kind regards from us all,
Yours faithfully,
J.A.Z. Murumbi
General Secretary, K.A.U.' "

Welsh Republicans of that time can take pride in that small gesture on their part towards speeding the end of an effete imperial regime in Kenya.

The editorial of Ifor Wilks is fully up to the high standard already achieved by him.

'Wales Wants the Truth', an incisive article of professional standard by Huw Davies investigates the financial and economic relationship between Wales and the 'rest of the United Kingdom'. He is also the author of a compelling piece, 'Problem y Ddwy Iaith yng Nghymru'.

On page 3, 'Crisis in West of Wales — 10,000 Welsh Workers Threatened', tells of the impending shut-down, 'for a start', of six hand-operated tinplate mills — 'at Morriston, Gowerton, Pontardawe, Llanelli and Burry Port', and of the London government's callous neglect and supreme indifference to the situation.

'Texts for Welshmen' — 1. Dr William Price, Leader of the Merthyr contingent in the Welsh Rebellion, 1839, and — 2. Capt. Owen Vaughan

*Cliff Bere
1949*

*Jord Pinault,
Breton (1951)*

*Bargoed Library & Bookshop.
Harri Webb in the shop entrance.
Eluned, Iwan and Cliff Bere in the house entrance.
(October 1951)*

Cardiff Eisteddfod 1960
Elis Evans, Harri Webb,
Gwyn with Cliff Bere, Eluned,
Gareth, Gwilym, Iwan

Cardiff Eisteddfod 1960
Eluned, Elis Evans,
Iwan, Gwilym, Gwyn, Gareth

Marriage of Huw and Eirwen Davies 1954

| Mudiad Gweriniaethol Cymru.
The Welsh Republican Movement.

DUPLICATE MEMBER-
SHIP CARD.

Name ....
Address ....
....
....
ASSOCIATE }
FULL } MEMBER
Joined ....
Recommended by
.... | **MUDIAD GWERINIAETHOL CYMRU**
THE WELSH REPUBLICAN MOVEMENT

ASSOCIATE
FULL } **MEMBERSHIP CARD**

of (Name) ....
(Address) ....
....
....
for period ....
(Signed) .... *for Council of W.R.M.*
PRIMARY AIM OF W.R.M.:
TO ESTABLISH A SOVEREIGN INDEPENDENT REPUBLIC OF WALES. |

Membership card

ENGLAND can force it on us
WALES has only 35 M.P.'s
ENGLAND nearly 600

They can bring back Tory Rule to Anti-Tory Wales. Labour Votes from WALES don't count at Westminster

Vote for Padley, Vote in Vain
Another Welsh Vote "down the drain"

Let Democracy be REAL in Wales

Let the Voters of Wales rule an Independent Government of Wales

HOME RULE alone can guarantee the Government our people want
VOTE

WELSH SOCIALIST
VOTE RADICAL,   VOTE REPUBLICAN

Vote ITHEL DAVIES
ITHEL DAVIES DROS OGWR, DROS GYMRU

Printed by the "Glamorgan Gazette" Ltd., Queen Street, Bridgend, and Published by C. Bere, 77 Nolton Street, Bridgend, Agent for the Candidate

Ithel Davies' election hand-out

A few of the Republican's publications

In Memoriam
of
Free Speech
who was crucified by the English Crown at Aberdare Police Court July 26 1950

An effective propaganda hand-out.

Delwyn a Lil Phillips

Let your motto be "ATTACK",
The Dragon stamping on the Jack;
To all Republicans far and near
Greetings for Christmas and New Year.
　　from Wales.

A Christmas card from Tom and Joyce.

MUDIAD GWERINIAETHOL CYMRU
THE WELSH REPUBLICAN MOVEMENT

A PUBLIC MEETING

Subject:--

A REPUBLIC FOR WALES

will be held at

on

CITIZENS OF WALES!
FORWARD TO THE WELSH REPUBLIC!

(writing in 1907), both speak of the great fighting traditions of the Welsh people.

The back page is all Harri Webb's own — 'Unconquered! — The Saga of Welsh Resistance', followed by No. 3 in his series — 'What they don't allow to be taught in Welsh Schools', which is about the Welsh Rebellion of 1839:

> " . . . A workers' army was built up to a strength estimated as sufficient to defeat the English troops in the South of Wales in open encounter, and to hold the Valleys as an independent Chartist Republic.
>
> " 'The long planned insurrection', wrote *The London Times*, 'deeply organised, managed with a secrecy truly amazing, was defeated only by concurrent act of Providence'.
>
> "But," adds Harri Webb, "the struggle itself did not end there! Today Welshmen still continue to fight for freedom and social justice. You are needed for it! Forge the Welsh Future and inherit the glory of the Welsh Past by joining the Welsh Republican Movement.
>
> "Write for details to: The Secretary, WRM, 144b, City Road, Cardiff."

And that was the new address from which *The Welsh Republican* was now published.

Chapter 15

'PLAN TO BLAST WATER LINE ALLEGED — Republican for Trial' ran the headline across the front page of *The South Wales Echo* newspaper on Friday, 27th February 1953 over its report of the committal by Caerdydd Stipendiary Magistrate, Mr Guy Sixsmith, of a member of the Welsh Republican Movement, Beriah Gwyndaf Evans, for trial at the next Assizes on a charge of possession of explosives with intent to cause serious injury to property in the United Kingdom and a further charge of possession of them giving rise to reasonable suspicion that they were for an unlawful object.

A statement made by the defendant in custody had said:

> "The reason I had the explosive material in my possession was that I did intend to do an individual attempt on the Birmingham water line. I felt that from a patriotic point of view it was time that something was done properly, that is, I suppose, from my own point of view."

The circumstances in which he had been arrested at his home in Clodien Avenue, Caerdydd a few days earlier were more reminiscent of a Hollywood film scenario than anything normally to be expected in a quiet suburban area. The police had closed the Avenue and its approach streets and had floodlit the allotments which at that time occupied the land to the rear of the Avenue's terraced houses. It was as if they were half expecting their quarry to 'make a break for it' in typical film story style. However, the Republican was enjoying a quiet evening at home with his wife and four children when Detective Superintendent Tom Holdsworth and Detective Chief-Inspector Harry Power, backed by a squad of their men, knocked on his door to say that they had a search warrant to look for explosives.

Gwyndaf, of course, at first denied that he had any such things in his house. But on being told that if necessary the house would be torn apart in the search for them, two sticks of gelignite and fifty detonators were eventually produced. He was arrested and taken into custody.

When Cliff Bere and Huw Davies went to see him the day after his arrest they were allowed to be taken to his cell accompanied by Detective Chief-Inspector Power on condition that no Welsh was to be spoken between visitors and prisoner.

"I don't want a lawyer," Gwyndaf said to his fellow Republicans.

"Yes, you do. We'll get you one — the best we can find," they told him.

They went at once to the office of a lawyer with a noted reputation for his skill in defence in criminal cases. They saw, not the man himself, but his partner, or assistant solicitor. After particulars of the case and the charges had been detailed to him with the help of a standard work on English criminal law which the Republicans had with them (he had shown a somewhat undue measure of surprise that laymen should presume to be so legally well-informed) he picked up the phone to get through to Detective Chief-Inspector Power. The fact that he seemed to be on very good, if not pally, terms with 'Harry' was slightly disconcerting to his two Republican visitors.

The need for a precautionary approach to the situation so far as they themselves too were concerned became a little more obvious again when the lawyer inquired of them with an almost studied casualness: "What are these sticks of explosive like, then? What size are they?"

"No idea — never seen that sort of thing," he was immediately told.

Before the end of the meeting he took a file from his shelves, saying, "Let's see if we can find who the judge will be taking the next Glamorgan Assizes here in Cardiff."

After a few moments perusal he looked up and gave his two listeners to understand that prospects were not looking very favourable. "We're not in luck; it will probably be Devlin," he said, "a quite recent appointment to the Bench." He then gave a graphic account of how the severity of the newly appointed Mr Justice Devlin's sentences was supposed to have caused people attending his courts to faint.

The two Republicans having, of course, no contrary information concerning the said judge available to them and feeling correspondingly saddened at the seemingly bleak prospects facing their imprisoned comrade, left the lawyer's office to return to Bargoed.

In the event, of course, Mr Justice Devlin proved to be one of the most decent and humane judges ever to sit on the English Judicial Bench; to which fact the outcome of this present case lends some testimony. A charitable explanation for the fact that the judge was so unjustly misrepresented may have been that of a lawyer's ploy in the hope of pulling two 'alarmed' men further into involvement with the facts of the case — to the possible advantage of the man he was being instructed to defend. On such faint hopes are the ploys of legaldom so often founded!

Within the next day or so after Gwyndaf's arrest came news that police searching for explosives had called at the home of a member of the WRM in Nantgarw, machine-tool operator Gwynfor Thomas. They had, of course, found nothing, even after going to the length of digging up the garden of his house.

* * *

At his trial in the Assize court in Caerdydd on the 13th March 1953 Beriah Gwyndaf Evans pleaded guilty to the charge of 'having in his possession two sticks of gelignite and fifty detonators with intent to cause serious injury to property in the United Kingdom.' The other charge was not proceeded with.

Mr John Rutter, Gwyndaf's defending counsel, made eloquent use of the hoary old story (in this instance completely untrue, as Gwyndaf was entirely his own man) of those lurking behind the scenes who had made use of the accused. "Evans," he said, "holds a certificate from the Home Office for his proficiency in the use of explosives. This may be one of the reasons why he became a tool in the hands of others."

Mr Justice Devlin told Gwyndaf: "You are perfectly right to tell me that you still adhere to your beliefs in this matter. You say that there should be a separate government for Wales, and you are entitled to bring that about by lawful means, but you are not entitled to further your beliefs by unlawful means. There are two courses I can take in this case. If you are willing to make an undertaking in this matter that you realize that you set about the furtherance of your objectives entirely in the wrong way and that you are now determined never to repeat this I shall make a probation order in your case."

The alternative, he told Gwyndaf, was that he would have to send him to prison for a long time.

Gwyndaf, in his wisdom, was glad to accept the judge's offer, and was placed on probation for two years.

Some of those 'behind the scenes lurking' Republicans who had been present in court listening to the proceedings, later that day picked up a copy of *The South Wales Echo* newspaper to read its report of the case, presented under a prominent front page headline, 'Republican's Promise to Judge'. But almost immediately, another, small heading over a report, 'Detonators Charge at Bangor', tucked alongside the account of the Assize court case drew their surprised attention.

It read:

> "Two hundred high explosive detonators, alleged to have been found in a sideboard at the lodgings of a Welsh Republican, were produced at a special magistrates' court at Bangor today.
>
> "Before the court was Peter Rhyswil Lewis, aged 29, of Penrallt, Bangor, charged with being in possession of the detonators for an unlawful object. He was defended by Mr D. Price White.
>
> "Lewis did not reply to the charge. He was remanded in custody until

March 20th.

"Lewis was stated to be a machine operator at an electrical factory at Bangor. He is a former student, it is understood, of Coleg Harlech and of the University College of North Wales, and spent some years as a merchant seaman.

"He is also understood to be an active member of the Welsh Republican Party."

At the remand hearing on 20th March he was bailed out of custody, against police wishes, by public spirited citizens, until on 14th May 1953 he was brought to trial at Caernarfon Assize Court. During these proceedings extensive reference was made to the Fron aqueduct explosion of the previous October. According to the London *Daily Herald* report of the case:

"Lewis said he would not have used the explosives in any way, and had nothing to do with the Rhaeadr explosion. He told Mr E.P. Wallis Jones prosecuting that the Welsh Republican Movement was a breakaway from the Welsh Nationalist Party, and was more socialist in its outlook. He denied that the Movement approved violence.

"Then Mr Wallis-Jones read an article from the Party's organ, *The Welsh Republican*. Referring to the Rhaeadr explosion, he said it spoke of the 'salutary terror created in English hearts by this display of Welsh striking power'.

"Lewis said this was comment on the news. He did not approve of it.

"Mr Justice Oliver: Do you think that this is praising violence? — Lewis: Not necessarily.

"The judge read further extracts from the editorial in the paper. One referred to a 'warm' welcome given to the queen on her Mid-Wales visit, and spoke of 'attempts being made to blow up the Fron aqueduct and apparently to block the Elan Valley road'.

"Another said the English authorities had been sent into a panic about the safety of the queen, and security measures had been rushed into effect.

"A third article said the men behind the explosion had 'faded away' into Welsh homes to strike again and again until the whole fabric of English rule had been shattered.

"Mr Justice Oliver commented: 'What is that but an incentive to violence, praise of violence and direct praise of the method to blow up the Rhaeadr dam?' "

Mr Emlyn Hooson, for the defence, said that it was Lewis and not the Republican Movement who was on trial. "This is a legal and not a political trial," he added.

The jury took a copy of *The Welsh Republican* which had commented on the Fron aqueduct explosion with them when they retired.

Pedr Lewis was found guilty and sentenced to 18 months imprisonment.

★ ★ ★

Addressing a rally at Bangor on 16th May, two days after Pedr Lewis had been sentenced, Mr Gwynfor Evans, President of Plaid Cymru said, as reported in *The Western Mail* under the heading 'Plaid Protests at Sentence of Welshman': "While we have made it perfectly clear that there are important differences in method and policy between the Welsh Republican group and the Welsh Nationalist Party, it is essential that we should express our indignation at the sentence which was imposed on this young man. His offence was precisely the same as that of a Republican in the South of Wales who was released after pleading guilty to the same charge, without any sentence at all . . . A sentence of 18 months upon this young man for having detonators in his possession is surely out of all proportion to the nature of the offence, and we are calling on the Home Secretary for his release."

Mr Gwynfor Evans also dealt with the 'standing down' of two jurors at Dolgellau Assizes the same week, and Mr Justice Oliver's subsequent statement that he would not be a party to putting a slight upon the Welsh people.

Mr Evans said:

> "In clearing himself of any accusation of malice towards the Welsh language the judge revealed the true situation in all its ugliness.
>
> "It is clear that no Welsh-speaking Welshman, if he is without English as a second language, has a place in the administration of justice in Wales. If an Englishman were to be put to the same test of a knowledge of a second language, 99 per cent of them would be shut out of the rights of jurors.
>
> "But this test is put only upon Welshmen. It is not to be found in any other part of the empire. It is quite clear that there is no remedy short of recognizing Welsh as the official language in courts of law in Wales."

Chapter 16

By the early Summer of 1953 the list of postal subscribers to *The Welsh Republican — Y Gweriniaethwr* numbered somewhere around the 300 mark. With the April-May 1953 issue Harri Webb had taken over the editorship from Ifor Wilks. Five issues of the paper had been produced under the able, at times inspired, direction of Ifor Wilks, and it was during this period, helped by the stirring events of the time, that the paper achieved some of its highest circulation figures. But now its care had passed into the hands of someone equally gifted with journalistic instinct and rich in knowledge of his nation's history. Harri Webb was to remain as Editor of *The Welsh Republican* for the next four years up to the time of its last issue.

'Welsh Trade Sabotaged' heads the front page of the April-May paper over Huw Davies' survey of economic matters. Two short excerpts suffice to tell the old, bitter, deceitful story. On *Coal* he says:

> "The miners had been upbraided with statements that the Welsh coalfield is subsidized by the English coalfields; that Wales draws more from the 'National Wages Pool' than she puts in; that absenteeism and unofficial strikes are leading back to local district agreements. Their critics overlook the basic fact that the Welsh coal industry has no control over its marketing. This means that coal which could be exported at world prices has been going under the 'double-pricing' system, at lower home-market prices to English consumers, thus providing an unrevealed subsidy to English industry. So-called losses on the Welsh production are not due to lack of productivity, but to the effect of this subsidy to England, deriving from an English based marketing policy."

And on *Tinplate* he says:

> "English imperialistic strategic interests have again triumphed over the basic needs of the Welsh worker. Mr Peter Thorneycroft, President of the Board of Trade (and incidentally one of the few Welsh Tory MPs), stated recently, 'I have been informed that a South Wales tinplate manufacturer was recently approached about the supply of

some 10,000 tons of tinplate, said to be required by the Chinese government. I have also heard that other inquiries for tinplate for China have been received by the tinplate industry. *The supply of tinplate would be contrary to our strategic controls.*' And 140 hand mills in South Wales are threatened with closure . . . "

(The Board of Trade seemed to operate under a different set of strategic controls over supply of armament materials, from England to Iraq, for instance, in later years.)

On that same page reference is made to the 'explosives' cases in the courts of Caerdydd and Bangor. Pedr Lewis was still on remand at times of publication. The opportunity was taken to draw attention to the Movement's Assistance Fund for helping patriots drawn into conflict with the forces of English Law.

An extract from Harri Webb's first editorial displays the inimitable style that was to adorn the paper's columns for the following years of its existence:

"In whose name do we Welsh Republicans speak? . . . We speak in the name of Wales and her people.

"For the time is coming when the people of Wales will arise and demand their rights. And take them. This is not wishful thinking. It is based on fact as unchallengable as Snowdon and as hard as anthracite. We do not deal in decayed and discredited doctrine.

"And because it is on these facts we stand, we face the future of Wales with confidence. Because it is the unconquerable soul of the Welsh people that we trust, we do not need to tout for the favours of the great. What better off is Wales for the energy and eloquence of Lloyd George or the brilliance and bounce of Aneurin Bevan? No, it is to the plain people we speak, and from whom we take inspiration: the plain people who marched with John Frost to Newport, or rode out with Rebecca against oppression, the country folk who for a generation fought the Tithe Wars against Queen Victoria's redcoats, the colliers who faced Churchill's bloody bayonets, and the women who kept house and family, yes and nation, together whilst the Christian gentlemen of England garrotted them with the Means Test."

The thoroughgoing commitment of the new Editor to his task is reflected in the diversity of subjects covered in this issue. An article in Welsh under the pen-name 'Alesandr' puts forward eminently practical-sounding suggestions as to the lines on which the constitution of a Welsh Republic could be shaped.

'Financial Correspondent — Exposing a Fraud' demonstrates effectively that it is *refusal* on the part of Maxwell Fyfe, 'Tory Demi-Minister for Wales', to publish details of the financial relationship between Wales and England, rather than the alleged impossibility of doing so, which witholds from the

Welsh people that vital information.

'Guilty Men' is reintroduced to the paper in this issue. Its subject is — "Lord Lloyd of Dolobran . . . Like his unlamented predecessor, David Llewellyn, Lord Lloyd is reported to be learning our language from gramophone records. Perhaps, after all, it would save trouble if the office of the English Minister for Welsh Affairs were permanently vested in a set of gramophone records, grinding out the same old comic songs which represent English policy in Wales — 'Rule Britannia', 'Soldiers of the Queen', and (not so comic) 'Buddy can you spare a dime?' "

And a new series is introduced — 'Who's Who in Wales'. No. 1 presented here is that mythical character, 'Dic Shon Dafydd'. But the promise is that to follow will be those whom we know, all too unfortunately, to exist as creatures of flesh and blood.

'Welsh Soldiers for Wales' is the title of an article, the burden of whose message goes: "This is not a plea for 'Welsh Units'. This is a demand for Welsh Armed Forces, stationed in Wales, trained in the unrivalled martial traditions of Wales and standing ready for the defence of Wales."

'An Open Letter to the Citizens of Cardiff' from Dr D.J. Davies of Pantybeiliau, Gilwern ends with this urgent plea:

> "You must get off the fence; must cease to bastardize yourselves with dedications of Churchill Ways and Marlborough Roads, and such trappings of English imperialist aggression; must move in a direction which is the very antithesis of the policy advocated by *The Western Mail* right in your midst. There is no future for Cardiff as a port or a great city or as Capital of Wales unless it identifies itself with the Welsh Nation and the fight for Welsh independence. As individuals and members of the city community, the security of Cardiff's citizens and Cardiff's aspirations to Capital status depends upon their being singlemindedly *Welsh*."

No. 4 of the series 'What they won't allow to be taught in Welsh Schools' recounts in succint brilliance the story of triumphs for the Welsh people in the Tithe Wars of last century — 'A triumph of lawlessness' — as bewailed by *The London Times*.

Finally, in 'Neither Red Flag nor Union Jack' Cliff Bere puts forward the case of The Welsh Republican Movement for unconditional independence.

> "It is the aim of The Welsh Republican Movement to establish the free Republic of Wales and, further, to establish the free Republic of Wales as a first rank nation.
>
> "The confidence of the Welsh Republican Movement in the quality — and therefore the world importance — of the Welsh people rests on

the well-established tradition of humanity and political maturity which is the heritage of our nation. Wales shall be a first rank nation, not by virtue of size or warpower or ethnological purity — but because of her political and social wisdom. That is the standard of true civilization.

"The Welsh Republican Movement has answered the question, 'What is a Welshman?', in the words: 'A Welshman is a citizen of Wales who — *no matter what his race or language or country of origin* — contributes to her welfare, maintains her best traditions and defends her rights and interests'. This definition is in accord with the great traditions of Welsh civilization which postulate that enmity between the common peoples of the nations is not innate, but is only engendered artificially by political means, such as the domination or exploitation of one nation or race by another.

"The Welsh Republican Movement is the uncompromising enemy of racialism, that is, of all and every doctrine which attempts to grade or judge nations and people by race or colour of skin. Racial tolerance is the hallmark of real civilization.

"In view of the recent manifestations of anti-Semitism in Russia, The Welsh Republican Movement finds it necessary to make its attitude towards them clear. There are significant facts to consider. It is generally recognized that the anti-Jewish riots or pogroms of Czarist Russia were fostered by Czarist policy to distract the attention of the people from the real cause of their miserable conditions. The Communists made great use of this fact in their early days. By today however it is plain that the Communist government of Russia in its turn is using the Jews as scapegoats. And even more overwhelmingly today than in pre-Revolution Russia, evidence suggests that the recurrent racial persecution is not due to any spontaneous enmity of the Russian people towards the Jews, but is the direct responsibility of the ruling hierarchy. The wheel has indeed turned full circle in Russia.

"Furthermore, it is logical to assume that a government which can perpetuate a tradition of anti-Semitism will also be ready to perpetuate a tradition of domination of subject nations. The despotic era of the czars saw nation after nation conquered and incorporated into the Russian Empire. With hardly one exception those nations remain today under the domination of the Moscow government. It is greatly significant that three subject nations of the old empire, i.e., Lithuania, Latvia, Esthonia which escaped and became self-governing again during the process of the revolution, have already been re-incorporated into the new-old empire of Russia. *The tradition of imperialism in a nation dies hard. No political doctrine will destroy it. Only the will of the subject nations to be free can do that.*

"Any grounds for believing that the victory of Communism in England would bring the freedom of Wales nearer are very uncertain. It could well lead to a worsening of the position. The only sure way forward to the self-governing Republic of the Welsh people is by the strength of their own tradition of civilization and the will of the people to be free. These, and these only, are the forces before which even the most strongly entrenched system of empire must at last yield and surrender."

★ ★ ★

The use of the address at 144b, City Road, Caerdydd from which *The Welsh Republican* was now published had been sub-let to the WRM by Mr Charles Owen who carried on a handicraft business there. Charles Owen, a former University student, and who hailed from the Llanrwst area, was a likeable young man with a burning ambition to make his way towards success in the world of business. Even though the tenancy arrangement with the Welsh Republican Movement was on a strictly business basis, there is a touch of irony perhaps, in that although he himself was of uncompromising conservative and private enterprise convictions he was more than willing to allow the use of his premises by those of an ideology so different from his own.

The reason for the very happy relationship between landlord and tenant, however, lay as much as anything with Charles Owen's staunch Welsh patriotism. The measure of this can best be judged by the fact that very soon after his acquaintanceship with the WRM began he stated his intention of publishing a news-sheet in Welsh in the style and format of *The Welsh Republican* and bearing the title of *Y Ceidwadwr*. Perhaps there was a slight sense of embarrassment on the part of the Republicans (quickly put aside, however), when he asked whether there would be any Republican objection if, for the printing of his project, he made use of the firm that printed *The Welsh Republican — Y Gweriniaethwr*. And so it came about that the loyal firm of Brook & Williams, Y Barri, printed two or three issues, at least, of *Y Ceidwadwr*, more or less concurrently with *Y Gweriniaethwr*.

And if the members of the Welsh Republican Movement found themselves able to embrace very little of the philosophy of the business and commercial world as expounded by Charles Owen in *Y Ceidwadwr*, then, for the fine, idiomatic and fluent Welsh language in which that paper was entirely written, they could find only admiration.

The Welsh Republican continued to be published from 144b, City Road for the next two years until the Spring of 1955. After that, its address for the remaining two years of its publication was 33, Charles Street, Caerdydd.

★ ★ ★

It was somewhere about this time, early Summer 1953, that occurred an incident, trivial and unimportant enough in itself, but centering as it did around the personality of Harri Webb and with elements of frustration and humour involved, well worth recounting.

Harri was back in Cymru. Huw Davies and Cliff Bere had come to meet him in Caerdydd on a Saturday, and equipped with necessary materials they were looking for a suitable site to stage the meeting they had in mind that would make a burningly memorable occasion of it for the citizens of Caerdydd.

A location was decided upon by mid-afternoon. The traffic along Queen Street opposite the junction with Churchill Way (it was long before the day of the pedestrian precinct) was probably not as heavy as on weekdays, and would allow a safe enough passage across to the centre of the road. Harri was to venture out there to begin speaking first, the others would of course go with him. But it would obviously be something of an ordeal for him, newly returned as he was from his comparatively peaceful book-lined sojourn in Cheltenham. He was game, however, and the urge to re-engage in memorable action was strong.

He was being nudged off the pavement to begin to make the crossing — he had a foot on the road — when from the pavement behind a man's voice on a loud note of surprise and excitement exclaimed: "Harri! how are you? Harri Webb!!" — and Harri, surprise mixed with what could well have been relief on his face, turned back from his bold venture into the stream of traffic to see the beaming face of a long lost friend from college days hurrying up with hand outstretched. Gladly Harri must have reached out to grasp it and allow himself to be hauled back to the safety and enthusiasm of what must surely have seemed to him at that moment something like a heaven-sent stroke of deliverance!

Then, whilst his Republican comrades fumed in chagrin and impatience, the nearby huddle of seemingly ecstatic reunion went on — and on — and on — until, by the time Harri's friend had released him, the flow of adrenalin mustered for Republican action had ebbed and almost all faded away. In subdued mood, backs turned on the busy road, the comrades headed for home — but alive and free and intent to fight another day.

Chapter 17

There was certainly irony, and inevitability too, perhaps, in the fact that it was in the month of the crowning of the English queen in June 1953 that *Y Gweriniaethwr* of the same date should rise to a new height of effectiveness in its timely statement of the Republican case for Cymru.

'An Old and Haughty Nation Proud in Arms' ran the front page headline quote from the poet John Milton. 'Our Duty — Defiance, Our Destiny — Deliverance', ran the sub-title, and went on:

"Many shadows have drifted across the hills of Wales and the people that holds them — the eagles of Rome, the ravens of the North, the vultures of London. But always we have stood firm. The Welsh people are, and the Welsh people shall be. Two thousand years of history cannot be shaken off like a dream, or analyzed away as a meaningless fable. Much of that history is dim and distant now. Many of its great figures are mere names. But what names! Rhodri and Cadwaladr, Hywel and Llywelyn, Owain Glyndŵr and Owain of the Red Hand. Such names as we are proud to give our sons; and with a right instinct, for these were our fathers who fought to preserve the inheritance which we in turn must pass on to our children.

"That inheritance is the land of Wales in all her stern beauty, with all the wealth of opportunity that the riches of her soil provide, her fish-crammed seas and sheep-crowded mountains, valleys flowing with milk, rocks bursting with coal, ports teeming with trade. All this at our feet, ours by right of birth. And all this in pawn, the cranes rusting over the empty quays, the water gathering in sealed-off seams, the drip of rain in silent quarries.

"But never the despair gathering in the heart or the rust in the brain. The great furnaces may be drawn, the proud chimneys fallen, the viaducts sold for scrap. Dowlais and Landore are deserts of sulphur and slag, but there is one fire that has never been slaked, one aspiration that has never been brought low, one crop that has never been blighted. That fire is the Welsh passion for a just society. That aspiration is the Welsh demand for a free people, that harvest must be the prosperity and security of our children, for which the Welsh people have fought since before the dawn of written history.

"For it was the Welsh people who took up the sword of their fallen princes, it was the Welsh people who kept in their hearts the wisdom of the old, abolished laws; it was the Welsh people who kept warm and living the songs that have inspired the longest resistance that history knows.

"If all this were mere mist and memory, there would be no Welsh Republican Movement today, you would not be reading these words . . . The Welsh Republican Movement reminds you, the Citizen of Wales, the heir to great things, that the final stage of that great struggle has yet to be faced, that there is no refuge in pious hopes, compromise politics or ostrich complacency. Our duty is to resist English aggression by any and every means. Our rewards will be to enter into our inheritance."

In the appropriately staider but no less purposeful tone of his editorial column the same writer reminds again:

The appearance of this number of *The Welsh Republican* coincides with the crowning of Queen Elizabeth II of England. This is not an event of any great historical importance, and has no relevance at all to Wales; but as it is receiving a certain amount of attention in the Press, we should be failing in our duty if we offered no comment.

"The whole ceremonial sums up to perfection the main tendencies in English society. Royalty is the ritual expression of Toryism at home and Imperialism abroad. Wales, on the other hand, has always upheld Socialism as opposed to Toryism, and Nationalism as opposed to Imperialism. We uphold the right of the individual to a decent life, and of the nation (any and every nation) to an independent existence. For unless the nation is free to order its own affairs, the individual's chance of a decent life is a thin one, as we in Wales know to our cost.

"Here today then, stand two nations, neighbours who could and should be good friends, but completely divorced in sentiment, for the one has followed evil courses and is rapidly harvesting the dire consequences. The other, our own, has never coveted an inch of any other people's land or a penny of other people's money. It may be that we too are soon to harvest the consequences.

"When one nation cherishes what another despises, it is useless to think of them as one unit. It would be folly to persist in a 'Union' which was imposed unilaterally by force and fraud, and which has never had any reality even on the football field. It would be criminal to acquiesce in the disastrous economic consequences of this 'Union' which have left such scars on our land. And this coronation, at which the Standard of Wales will be carried in Westminster Abbey by the chairman of the Midland Bank will, we hope, be the last opportunity which anyone will have of hailing an English monarch as sovereign of Wales."

But it was in verse that the case for a Republican Wales found on this occasion its most telling and moving expression. Set like a gem in the centre of the striking front page is Harri Webb's poem:

A LOYAL ADDRESS TO WALES

Queen of the rains and sorrows,
   Of the steep and broken ways,
The pledge of our tomorrows
   Redeems your sunless days.

Queen of the gorse and heather,
   Of the upraised, unhewn stone,
Queen of the bitter weather,
   We kneel before your throne.

Take us, there is no other
   At whose feet we would offer our pride;
Take us and break us, O Mother
   For whom our fathers died.

While your eyes yet know not laughter,
   While your lips but speak of pain,
All other tasks come after,
   All other loves are vain.

Queen of the sunken valleys,
Queen of the gates of the sea,
Rise up to the voice that rallies
The vanguard of the free.

When the night of the grey Iscariots
Lies dead in the red of the morn,
Queen of the scythe-wheeled chariots!
Rise up, ride out, reborn.

'*Brenhines Pwy? — Cur Hen y Coroni*' yw pennawd llith fach gan Huw Davies sy'n diweddu fel hyn:

"*Nid yw'r goron Seisnig ond arwydd o'n colledion ni fel cenedl. Cynrychioli Lloegr, a'i diwylliant, a'r ymerodraeth, a'r gwledydd a*

> *dyfodd dan arweiniad Lloegr y mae'r 'Teulu Brenhinol'. Nid yw'n perthyn i Gymru. Teulu Seisnig ydyw, a'i dras yn Almaenaidd. Collodd Cymru ei thraddodiad brenhinol ei hun ers canrifoedd. Yn awr, Gwerinbobl Cymru yw cynheiliaid ein cenedl, ac i Gymru y mae ein teyrngarwch ni'n ddyledus. Gallwn ddathlu 1953 orau gan ymroddi o'r newydd i achos annibyniaeth ein gwlad a'n pobl. Felly y symudwn ni'r anghyfiawnder â Chymru a olygir gan yr oruchwyliaeth frenhinol Seisnig."*

And, very appropriately, this issue has for the subject of its 'Guilty Man' non other than Henry Tudor " . . . who became King Henry VII of England . . . dead a long time. But his influence and example are still alive in Wales. For he was the first of the London Welsh careerists to go to town in a big way. He led a Welsh army to victory against the English and told them that they would regain their ancient liberties by putting a Welshman on the English throne. Then he forgot all about Wales and devoted his great talents to strengthening English power . . .

"His son was the notorious Henry VIII about whom even English historians find it difficult to enthuse . . .

"One more generation and we are done with this brief dynasty. Edward VI, a pathetic nonentity; Mary I, known in English history as 'Bloody Mary'; and Elizabeth I, known in Irish history as 'Bloody Elizabeth'. With this barren and embittered woman the House of Tudor came to an end.

"It is fitting that the sickening cant about 'a new Elizabethan age' be left to modern Welsh lickspittles and time-servers and that the stark truth of history be remembered by all good Welsh people."

'Welsh Law for Wales' is the title of an impressive article by 'a young Welsh lawyer who has made a special study of the old laws of Wales' (it does not tax the imagination to divine who this young lawyer might be).

> "In stressing the ethical basis of law the Welsh lawyer was heartily expressing an inherent element in the spirit of the Welsh. He had no choice. Throughout the ages the consistent battling for the ideal of a just society has marked us off from other people; it has formed and unified our national consciousness. The maxims of Welsh jurisprudence — the revolt of Glyndŵr — the Rebecca Rising — the nationhood of Nonconformity — the triumph of the Welsh Labour Movement, these are the milestones that stand out boldly along the road of the Welsh nation in its forward march.
>
> "For over six hundred years Welsh nationhood has had to submit not only to an alien political culture, but also to a legal pattern which is foreign and hostile to the traditional sense of the Welsh community. It is dangerously easy for us to forget that English jurisprudence is only suited to that nation and its offspring, and no other. For what has been

the purpose of English law? Until recent years, English law knew one purpose, and that was the 'practical one' of being subservient to the prosperity and interests of the burghers and nobles. Consequently, the process of English legal evolution is the result of the struggle of interests. The courts were not concerned with ethical interpretation. Half a century past, the English judge Buckly could say, 'This court is not a court of conscience', to which his cousin Lord Sumner would agree, 'We are not free to administer that vague jurisprudence which is sometimes attractively styled as justice between man and man.' This view, that lawyers are concerned with a 'positive law' without regard to its resultant goodness or badness, has coloured the entire English attitude to law. Of course, it became a comfortable gospel of a nation that was thrusting out on colonial adventures and had the whole world at its feet. It allowed the governing class the right to exert itself freely at the expense of the less fortunate; it sanctioned the exploitation of nation by nation. 'This court is not a court of conscience.'

" . . . The age demands that the sense of right shall produce the law, and not law a sense of right. To deny this demand is to court bloodshed, as in Malaya and Kenya.

"Here then is our point of contact with the principles of Welsh jurisprudence. Its centuries of tradition have not been meaningless. For at this source — in the writings of Blegywryd and Iorwerth ap Madog — there resides the strongest hope of discovering a basis upon which we can build new precepts to meet the social and national needs of a self-governing Wales."

This notable and timely issue of *The Welsh Republican* ends with the subject of 'Our National Anthem'.

"1858 was not a year in which Wales had much to sing about. The great Risings were a memory, the great Strikes were still to come. Rebecca had ridden home, Frost and his Chartists were convicts in exile and Dic Penderyn lay in his felon's grave. Disillusion and apathy seemed to rule. But in Pontypridd there lived two working men, a father and a son, EVAN JAMES and JAMES JAMES. Together they composed a song for a local Eisteddfod — the song we know and the world knows as our National Anthem: *'Hen Wlad fy Nhadau'*. For within two years this tremendous hymn of affirmation had been accepted by the Welsh people as their true voice. Not many nations can claim that their Anthem has risen from the common people and been adopted by unanimous acclaim. But Wales is like that. No Court Musicians, no royal patronage, no propaganda machine, no culture —

pumping by expensively subsidized committees. The people had spoken.

"English and quisling-Welsh reaction was typical. A moderate man was found to compose a rival 'Anthem' emphasizing Welsh 'Loyalty' (to England), the insipid 'God Bless the Prince of Wales'. Now comes one of the best jokes in Welsh history. For no sooner had God been incited to bless The Prince of Wales than the gentleman became involved in a sordid gambling scandal which hit the headlines in a big way. (You will not read about this in the glamourized biographies of English royalty now being penned by hired hacks, but you will find it in more responsible history books.) That, at any rate, was the end of the 'rival anthem'. The Welsh people preferred to praise the Land of the Fathers than to pray for a profligate German princeling. Today there is only one Anthem for Wales and only one loyalty for her people. "When next you rise to your feet for 'Hen Wlad fy Nhadau' remember the strength and splendour of the people from whom it sprang; remember that their battle goes on.
YOU ARE NEEDED FOR IT!"

* * *

Y Gweriniaethwr had by now established itself as a notable and very readable organ of political propaganda. Its reputation had long since spread beyond the confines of Cymru; the fact that it was as well-known and appreciated in the sister Celtic countries as it was, could only redound to the credit and honour of the country of its origin.

There was indeed, great interest shown in the paper on all sides, and not only from those on the side of freedom for nations still under domination by others. Information from well-nigh unimpeachable sources had long since come to the knowledge of the WRM that the authorities had given very serious consideration towards finding some pretext for proscribing the Movement and its paper. But, for the present, the regular and encouraging refrain coming through the post concerning the paper was — 'where to get it?' — 'where could it be bought?'

But if *The Welsh Republican* was going from strength to strength under dynamic editorship, from another aspect the Movement's activities were abating. With the imprisonment of Pedr Lewis, the northern branch had lost the presence of an important co-ordinator there. The Abertawe region had lapsed into barely more than sporadic activity. The situation in the Caerdydd area was much the same.

In Bargoed, economic necessity had driven Cliff Bere, in the most literal sense of the term, underground. He was now working the afternoon/evening shift at the coalface and the notorious new 'drivage' in Ogilvy colliery at Deri, a few miles further up the valley from Bargoed. It was an experience which he was not entirely unprepared for and unaccustomed to; a few years before he had worked similarly at the coalface in Lady Windsor colliery in Ynysybŵl.

Huw Davies was sometimes occupied with his sporting activities on Saturday afternoon, and this meant that the old freedom to sally out together to the Saturday venues for meetings in the valley towns had become more restricted. As a result, *The Welsh Republican* paper was coming to assume an increasingly important rôle in Movement affairs.

The editorial of the August-September 1953 issue of the paper begins on this high note of confidence:

> "With this number of *The Welsh Republican* we begin our fourth Volume. During the last three years we have had the satisfaction of seeing a gradual transformation in the Welsh scene, and a retrospective glance may help us to understand the nature of this change and to appreciate the pattern of the future.
>
> "The Welsh Republican Movement took official shape in the immediate post-war period, when two outstanding facts forced themselves on the consciousness of all who were ready to work for Wales. The most important of these facts was the abandonment by the Labour Party of a Welsh Home Rule policy. This represented a betrayal of one of the fundamental doctrines of Socialism by an organization which since 1945 has been dazzled by the prospect of becoming the second party in the English State. Gradually there has developed in that party a difference of opinion, which in the course of time will amount to an open schism: the difference between the purblind careerists who wish to maintain the exploitation of Welsh resources and labour by English imperialism, and on the other hand the genuine socialists and patriots who believe in a free Wales."

It ends:

> "We have had our reward. The tempo has quickened. Under the stimulus of competition both Plaid Cymru and the Welsh Labour Movement have improved out of all recognition, whilst the renegades have been driven to hysterical excesses of self-justification that only further reveal their unfathomable baseness.
>
> "Meanwhile the Welsh Republicans drive forward. There is no need to remind our readers of the numerous occasions on which a hostile press has been reluctantly compelled to devote its headlines to the activities of the forces working for Welsh independence. Welsh

Republican literature has permeated the whole community. Our public meetings have been notable and our speakers everywhere favourably received. Not concerned with grinding any axe but the one that will be laid to the roots of English rule, the Movement gains in strength and influence. The future beckons the Free Independent Welsh People."

On the front page, under the heading 'Release Peter Lewis!' the paper repeats its urgent appeal on behalf of Lewis. 'Trial by Prejudice', it maintains: " . . . So a recognised worker for Welsh self-government was tried in Wales by English law, before a judge steeped as all his ilk in the most conservative traditions of the English State. This judge was under criticism at the time for anti-Welsh prejudice, and also made extraordinary remarks about the Welsh Republicans in the trial.

"Once sentenced, Peter Lewis was treated as a common felon. Essentially a political prisoner, he is jailed with the socially outcast, as if guilty of robbery with violence, or worse. This despite his known high character, his fine idealism and the devoted religious background of his family. He is forbidden an appeal, possibly by the very judge who sentenced him.

"*The Welsh Republican* calls on Welsh Citizens to condemn this treatment for the scandalous injustice it is. Action by the Welsh MPs at Westminster, particularly by Mr Goronwy Roberts, Labour and Home Rule MP for Caernarfon, by the Chairman of the Council for Wales, and by all, should bring pressure on the government Minister generally responsible, Sir David Maxwell Fyfe. *Let Peter Lewis Go Free Forthwith!*"

The back page is headlined 'Take the Brake off Welsh Transport', over a well-informed article on the England orientated travel routes in Wales. It ends in that generations-long, more than ever urgent cry:

> "What Wales needs is good *internal* communications, and chiefly that great central highway from Cardiff to Holyhead. It has been planned by Welshmen with vision and knowledge. But until we gain independence it will remain a dream.
>
> "Its tourist value alone could be considerable. Look what the Antrim Coast Road means to Northern Ireland in this respect. And what has Northern Ireland got that Wales hasn't got? (Except perhaps a certain measure of Home Rule!) The immense resources of mid-Wales in industries auxiliary to forestry and agriculture are doomed to rot whilst this road remains unbuilt. The chaos of the Welsh road system remains a symbol of the state of the nation — and of any nation ruled by another — the Road to Ruin."

Webb's potted history item is about the long heroic struggle of the Quarrymen of the North to establish, first, The North Wales Quarrymen's

Union in 1874, and then, via strike and suffering, against the tyranny of the quarry owners, their right to juster conditions of work and reward for their onerous, dangerous toil.

Chapter 18

In the October-November 1953 issue of the paper, under the bold front page headline 'No False Freedom for Wales' an article over the name of Gwilym Prys Dafis presents an analysis of the Parliament for Wales Campaign then in process of organization.

'Devolution, Federalism or *Independence?*' it asks, and begins:

> "The choice before those Welshmen and Scotsmen who have been working intermittently since the Cambro-Scottish Home Rule Conference of 1890 for an Association of British States is between the federal principle and the devolutionary. However, this must be made clear: devolution is different in all respects from federalism. 'Devolution' and 'federalism' are not synonymous. For the principle paramount in federalism, partnership — the general and the regional government each within its sphere co-ordinate and independent — gives place in devolution to considerations issuing from the regional government being subordinate to the general."

It went on, under a sub-heading, 'Belfast on Taff?' —

> "After months of highsounding propaganda the current Parliament for Wales Campaign has accepted the devolution principle as fundamental. Hence we read: 'In general the arrangement would resemble those which operate in Northern Ireland'. The constitution of the Parliament of Northern Ireland rests on the Government of Ireland Act, 1920, which contains the following crucial proviso: 'Notwithstanding the establishment of the Parliament of Northern Ireland . . . or anything contained in this Act, the supreme authority of the Parliament of the United Kingdom shall remain unaffected and undiminished over all persons, matters and things in Ireland . . .'

> "The Government of Ireland Act is in many respects a striking testimonial to the value of devolution as a means of preserving the existent system of unitary government. Behind 'the arrangements in Northern Ireland', as any Lloyd George knows, every influence of the old guard is arrayed.

"Are we then really to believe that a Welsh Parliament modelled on the Irish arrangement could arise supreme with the challenge of a Welsh renaissance to change materially the centuries-old course of national disintegration?"

It concludes in challenging style:

"Having accepted devolution as the basis of its proposal, the Campaign Committee is paralyzed into surrendering to London all control over the most vital matters with which governments have to deal: PEACE and WAR. If a parliament is to be denied any influence over such matters, what, we may ask, is the prospect?

"Welsh Republicans take the simple view that the key to effective government is the vesting of power in government. We therefore say that if a Welsh Parliament is to be a reality it must possess power to act independently of, and, if need be, in opposition to the London Parliament. The Government of Ireland Act, 1920, is certainly not a source of that power."

On that same front page a brief but potent item of celebration is set to catch the eye:

"ANNIVERSARY
October 19th 1953
In grateful commemoration of the unknown patriots
who last year struck a blow for Wales at the
Fron Aqueduct, Radnorshire.

And on another page in timely accord, under the title 'The Rape of Rhayader' is the poignant story of William Lloyd, Casnewydd (*Newport*):

"I am enclosing the story of Rhayader as I often heard it repeated by my father. Often, as a child, I listened to the following narrative. For years beyond memory the valleys and hills in and around Rhayader rang with the voices of the Lloyd family. The hills and quarries trembled with the shots fired by that old family of quarrymen. The old foot lathes whirred, as often other members of the family carried on the ancient craft of wood-turning, manufacturing wheel-stooks for farm carts and other rolling stock. Their craft was known throughout Wales. They were a happy and contented family. But a blow was to fall which staggered that old Welsh family, and caused the rebel blood in the veins of the younger Lloyds to throb.

"The march of English development came to the peaceful vales of Rhayader. The Birmingham Waterworks were to be established, whether or not sorrow, hardship and poverty came to the people of Rhayader. That did not matter. Nothing could halt the English corporation's request for water. The ancient cottage of the Lloyds stood in the path of the onslaught. It had to be removed. First came a request to the Lloyds to move; then pressure. But the Lloyds stood fast. They refused to give away the only property they owned. Then the English authorities bared their fangs. The Lloyds had to be removed. With force if necessary.

"The thugs arrived, supported by every means at the disposal of their English masters. But the Lloyds did not give up without a struggle. They fought back and gave a good account of themselves. But eventually the family was forcibly evicted. The family had fought well, but lost. Their home had gone, but not their Welsh spirit. For days they lived in the open and watched with sorrow their home being torn down. The family camped on the Black Mountains to discuss the future.

"The family separated, some to Hereford, some to Newport, while a few of the younger Lloyds went so far as Canada and Australia. But the never-dying spirit of the Lloyds lived on. Wherever they wandered they continued to fight the cause of all Welshmen, for Freedom from the chains of tyranny from England which binds Welshmen to Poverty, Want, Unemployment, Injustice, aye, and War."

There are two significant quotes under the heading 'Sayings for Welshmen':

1. "The persistence of the Welsh language is no miracle. It is an expression of the vitality which has defeated every imaginable adverse circumstance. The Welsh people are a tough people. They may be outnumbered, but not overwhelmed. The most important element in Wales is Y WERIN — the common people, and so long as the young of Wales recognise and respect the great qualities of their own common folk, Wales will not only survive, but will contribute at the highest level to the thought and life of the world." (Goronwy Roberts, Labour and Home Rule MP for Caernarfon).

2. "I admit, gladly and willingly, that a people charged with the care of its own destiny achieves thereby a spaciousness not otherwise capable of being obtained. Self-respect, exhilaration, creativeness — all these seem to be the definite outcome of self-government." (Harold Laski — 'Nationalism and the Future of Civilization').

In 'Great Events — Great Places' a Special Correspondent tells the story of how "In February 1804, at Merthyr Tydfil, Trevethick's steam locomotive pulled the first locomotive train in the history of the world . . . It happened at Penydarren on 13th February 1804. From then on it was easy — The Rocket, Puffing Billy, Canadian Pacific, Trans-Siberian, Golden Arrow, it all started under the slag heaps of Dowlais Top.

"We cannot claim that the inventor of the steam railway, Richard Trevethick, was a Welshman, though he was the next best thing, Cornish, and probably understood a language very like Welsh . . .

"To commemorate a great event that took place at the dawn of the modern age would today be to reaffirm a belief in the genius and destiny of the Welsh people, those unknown Joneses and Evanses who translated Trevethick's dream into practical application, and whose descendants can forge an equally worthy future that will banish the shadows of the immediate past. 'A city that is built on a hill cannot be hid.' "

The inimitable Webbian potted history in this issue is of the Cardiff Dock Strike of 1911:

" . . . Seamen, tippers, coal-trimmers and railwaymen co-operated in a disciplined, unbreakable body. The strike funds were swelled by thousands of donations from Cardiff's ordinary people . . . The beginning of the strike was announced by rockets fired from the Docks. Answering rockets were fired from Penarth, Barry, Port Talbot and Swansea. The blockade was complete. The shipowners retaliated savagely. There was violence in the streets. Blacklegs were rushed in from England, but a brilliant intelligence system frustrated all these moves. Ship hawsers were stretched across strategic roads. Picket boats were sunk. Not a blackleg got through. Strike leaders were jailed. Workers stormed the City Hall. The port of Cardiff, third port of the world, centre of the coal trade, stood still. The only ships the strike committee allowed in were trawlers with fish for the hospitals, and those carrying newsprint for a sympathetic newspaper (*not* The Western Mail!). At last the owners had to negotiate and concede a living wage. Men of all races, languages and colours took part in this struggle which had all the precision of a military operation, all the fire of a crusade. So they earned for themselves and their children the heritage of that Welsh Citizenship which is based on justice and democracy.

"Today Cardiff Docks are empty. Depression, not coaldust is the menacing cloud. The struggle goes on.
YOU ARE NEEDED FOR IT!"

★ ★ ★

As already mentioned, Harri Webb was back in the Land of His Fathers. His formidable Republican presence was now installed in charge at the Public Library in Dowlais, putting all his talents and knowledge available at close hand once more at the service of his own people. It was an office he was to hold for many happy, fruitful years to come.

But if one pillar of the old Bargoed establishment had returned — at least, to very close and convenient proximity to the old HQ — another pillar was soon to be lost. Huw Davies' selfless, unsparing dedication to the work and aims of the Welsh Republican Movement was an inspiration to those working with him. However, as already made clear, he was certainly not a man with interests confined to the pursuit of matters political only. And by now, as he grew into his late twenties, there were, his sporting interests apart, other considerations also demanding his attention. The idea of settling down to life in an environment more of his own making was obviously an attraction to him. Anyway, in the Autumn of 1953 Huw moved back to live in Caerdydd. Not many months later he had married Eirwen, the obvious and lovely source of that attraction.

He maintained his wholehearted involvement with the WRM throughout the following three and a half years of publication of *The Welsh Republican*.

★ ★ ★

In the Autumn of 1953 the Breton patriot Andre Geoffroy was still in prison. But freedom for him at last was not to be long delayed. There is in the following excerpt from a letter dated 26th July 1993 to this writer a reminder of the success of the efforts made on his behalf by so many in many countries, amongst whom the name of Huw Davies has a very honourable place:

"I am interested to know of the work you have undertaken. Andre Geoffroy died a good few years ago; and I do not know of the whereabouts of his family. As you presumed, he was released shortly after the international campaign on his behalf. After his release he lived in various parts of France, but never could get rid of the traumas he suffered.

"His story, and especially that of his emprisonment, was related at length in a book published by Ronan Carlcou and called 'Au village des condamnés à mort'. The publisher was 'Les Editions de la Table Ronde' (Paris). It is based on the prison journal Geoffroy kept. The National Library of Wales may have a copy of it.

"I met Geoffroy in Brest, where he was temporarily working, sometime in 1956/57. I think he took to drink, as he was separated from his family for a long time and was living a very lonely life . . .

Ganoc'h a galon,
Yann Fouéré"

★ ★ ★

A piece by Cliff Bere in the December 1953-January 1954 *Welsh Republican* is perhaps suggestive of the slant Republican thinking was beginning to take at this time. Under the heading 'Nightmare in Toryland' it says, amongst other things:

"For English toryism the Welsh Nation has always been, as it were, a skeleton in the cupboard of the English house. Hitherto they have tried to banish it by ignoring it. But the new militancy in Wales tells them emphatically that they have failed.

"And now the concentration of police attention is a symptom of the very real fear besetting toryism — namely the fear that the Welsh Labour Movement and the Welsh Nationalist Movement will turn towards each other and move forward, united and irresistible, to their inseparable aims. For only self-government will bring the Welsh people the government they want and vote for. 27 of the 36 Welsh MPs are returned by Labour. Yet tory government is our lot in Wales today. Only self-government can put an end to that situation.

"The prospect of this realization taking general hold in Wales (already at least 6 Welsh MPs support the current Parliament for Wales campaign) is the nightmare of the tories. They are hell-bent to stop it. For, they reason, even though solidly and militantly Labour, Wales can always be kept in harness to England and controlled by political or — if necessary — police methods, so long as she remains part of the English system. But Wales self-governing means Wales lost to tory England for ever.

"Tory political efforts in Wales are therefore concentrated upon one main purpose — that is, to keep the National Movement and the Labour Movement in Wales apart.

"This aim and the dire anxiety behind it stands revealed in the columns of the tory press in Wales, and in the utterances of the tory Minister for Welsh Affairs when invoking the collaboration of Welsh Labour in his work in Wales which is 'above politics'. That is hypocrisy of a large order — even for a tory. But English toryism will use every means of fraud and force to keep its grip on Wales. It is only the united strength of the National and Labour Movements of Wales that will cast it off forever."

At about this time Bere accompanied Webb on a visit to the home of S.O. Davies, MP for Merthyr Tydfil. That evening Harri was to deliver an address on the martyrdom of Dic Penderyn to a gathering of Trade Union and Labour Party members in Merthyr. A happy little memory of the occasion which mischievously refuses to fade is of the imperturbable Webb's wholehearted attack on and substantial demolition of a large chocolate cream gateau at the teatable in the MP's house shortly before the meeting, whilst a delighted Mrs Seph Davies looked on in admiration and astonishment.

The meeting was a great success and warm tributes were paid to the speaker from amongst the large audience for his eloquent and stirring account of the Penderyn story. (This was later to be published in pamphlet form by Gwasg Penderyn, Lôn Coed Brân, Abertawe.)

Some six at least of the Welsh Labour MPs were firmly committed Home Rule supporters, and by now quite a few members of the WRM had also enrolled as members of the Labour Party in their respective localities as a step towards forming a national unity of resistance to Tory colonial government of Wales. A Welsh Republican Movement Council member, Haydn Jones, fought local government elections under the Labour label in both the Ffynhonnau and Y Mwmbls Wards in Abertawe.

On the front page of that current issue of *The Welsh Republican* that theme of 'Resistance' was firmly stated in C.B.'s brief piece:

> "The future of Wales depends on the success and speed with which we can re-establish as a living force the great tradition of militant resistance to national subjection. Such a tradition is as vital to Wales now in her struggle for freedom as breath to the human body.
>
> "It is the living tradition of endeavours and sacrifices made for a nation which inspires its youth in each new generation and sustains them in the lonely hours of their own endeavour and sacrifice.
>
> "The struggle of the Welsh Nation to live shines, heroic and unremitting through the records of history. England's efforts, no less unremitting, have been to make that tradition of Welsh resistance to national subjection a dead tradition. England has ignored and distorted Welsh history, suppressed facts, slandered, ransacked the repertoire of deceit to undermine the national pride and self-reliance of the Welsh people. It is small wonder that in the minds of some Welshmen the tradition of resistance to national subjection lies broken.
>
> "The purpose of the Welsh Republican Movement, through the medium of deed and word, is to resurrect the great tradition of militant nationalism in the minds of all Welsh men and women."

On page 2, alongside a fine editorial, Huw Davies, under the heading 'Smile — Smother — Swindle', once again directs his incisive attack against 'The Technique of English Tory Policy in Wales':

> " . . . Contributors to *The Welsh Republican* have many times discussed the attitude of the English Conservative government to

Welsh calls for information. Both R.A. Butler and Maxwell Fyfe, albeit with expressions of goodwill and sympathy, have, for example, refused to make any arrangements even to review the facts regarding the revenue collected from Wales. Similarly, the War Office declines even to consider demands for the organization of conscripted Welshmen into integrated Welsh Armed Forces. Yet, here we have two of the most important activities of the English government in Wales, the collection of revenue and the conscription of Defence Manpower. Wales can pay her taxes; her sons may be sent to British Guiana, or wherever else the English Imperial Order is in danger; but not an atom of consideration will she get for her plea for at least an account of these actions . . . "

On another page, 'Wales First' by 'Deeside' with reference to 'recent coronation junketings' and talk of 'Our new Elizabethan Age' ends with:

"Welsh Republicans have a straight answer to this stuff. We do not recognise ourselves as participants in 'your' tradition. We repudiate your 'island story', your monarchy, your Elizabethan Age, and your Westminster. Our loyalty is to *our* way of life, our people, our country and *our* New Age. The English can keep their ways for all we care. We demand the right to follow *our* way."

And alongside, Gwilym Prys Dafis relates in succinct and stirring style the story of the Quarrymen of our North — 'A Heroic Story of Welsh Labour':

" '*Gorthrwm, llygredigaeth ac anonestrwydd roddes fod i'r Undeb*', so wrote one of the founders of the North Wales Quarrymen's Union," Gwilym begins.

Then in a telling chapter illustrating so well the heroism of that struggle, he writes:

"The masters of Penrhyn, Dinorwig, Glynrhonwy and Chwarel Fawr, despite the warning of 1874, were in no temper to accept the principle of Unionism. They let things drift along a few years. But before the century was out, Lord Penrhyn threw the final challenge. 'Where can you find in any act of Parliament anything which compels an employer of labour to recognize the authority of a committee which seeks to interfere with direct communication between employer and employed?'

"To this rigmarole the men retorted pointedly, 'Shall we have your lordship's reply to the question of the right of one to make his matter a matter concerning all?' And that in a nutshell is the essence of Unionism. October 1896 came, and the battle was on between the lordship of Penrhyn and his 3,000 quarrymen for the recognition of

Unionism. *'We shall press until we are even in want of bread before we shall give in on the question of combination,'* declared the twenty-two year old Union.

"Throughout that dark and bleak winter, week followed week, month followed month. The men of Cae-Braich-y-Cefn, Penrhyn stood their ground, until the Spring sunshine of 1897 heralded the coming of a new season. Undeb Chwarelwyr Gogledd Cymru had proved itself in the fire of battle."

And Harri Webb's splendid contribution on the back page of this fine issue needs no excuse for its inclusion here in its entirety. Under its great block heading, 'NEMESIS', it reads:

" 'I vow to thee my country, all earthly things above,
Entire and whole and perfect, the service of my love,
The love that asks no questions, the love that stands the test,
That lays upon the altar the dearest and the best.'

"We cannot but respect the writer of those lines. He was Cecil Spring Rice, English Ambassador to the USA in World War I. And yet, what service to his country was he forced to perform? For his story crosses with that of another patriot, from another country, who was also possessed by:

" 'The love that never falters, the love that pays the price,
The love that makes undaunted the final sacrifice.'

"That man was Roger Casement of Ireland.

"His work for Ireland led him to the gallows. But many in England understood Casement's motives and Ireland's unanswerable case, and petitioned for clemency. But they were assailed by rumours that Casement, far from being the upright character everyone thought him, was in fact a sexual pervert of vilest order. They refused to be convinced and pointed out that in the past, the English government itself had staked its reputation on his personal integrity. Then a diary was produced, alleged to be Casement's. It was so obscene and revolting that sympathy was silenced and Casement was duly hanged.

"But that diary was a forgery produced in the murky cellars of Scotland Yard. Dennis Gwyn, Casement's biographer, has made the charge, and Dr Maloney has pieced the sordid story together, and it has not been denied because it cannot be denied. So much for the famous English decency. Filth and lies forged by the police themselves so that one man might hang. And Spring Rice, the author of the noble lines quoted above, had to spread these stories in America, knowing them to be untrue. His, indeed, was a love that asks no questions.

"But, as we have said before in these pages, the gods are just. English public opinion today is sorely troubled by the vices of which Casement was falsely accused.

"Viscount Samuel, the distinguished elder statesman has risen in the most solemn session of Parliament to declare his distress at 'the vices of Sodom and Gomorrah in our midst' and to speak of 'retribution'.

"Yes, retribution it is. For Casement and all the other murdered patriots and plundered nations. A country which has respected the rights of no other community must in the end cease to respect itself. A country which has based its politics on the negation of morality now sees its own internal morality crumbling away. For Welsh patriots, firm on the unageing rock of decent and democratic standards, the future is clear. For England, in the tremendous words of Yeats: 'THE GHOST OF ROGER CASEMENT IS BEATING ON THE DOOR'."

Chapter 19

The Welsh Republican Movement faced into 1954 with the dedicated nucleus of those who had been mainly responsible for directing its operations from its valley base dispersed. By now, only Cliff and Eluned Bere and their young family remained as permanent custodians of that onetime so vibrant HQ, although Harri Webb, Huw Davies and others were frequent callers in connection with Movement affairs. It was Harri Webb and Huw Davies, in fact, who took upon themselves the main responsibility for keeping in good and efficient order the always increasing register of postal subscribers to *The Welsh Republican*. The work of despatching the paper on its two-monthly appearances continued to be done from Bargoed.

The editorial of the February-March 1954 issue is a statement of the Welsh Republican Movement philosophy and policy, so noteworthy, and incidentally so apposite to the situation in this later day, as to justify its inclusion here in full without further comment.

> "It is not the business of the Welsh Republican Movement to defend itself. We exist to attack and to focus the attacking spirit of our nation. Some of our readers, however, may wish to provide themselves with arguments against the criticism that Welsh patriots are parochial-minded and anti-English.
>
> "The basis of our philosophy is *National*. Our historical analysis leads us to the self-evident proposition that Nationalism, be it for an ancient civilized country like Wales, or an emergent community in Asia or Africa, is the challenging, creative force of our time. This in itself redeems our attitude from provincialism and the mind turned in on itself. The sea that washes the shores of Wales encircles the whole earth. What we do in Wales today for our own deliverance is part of a universal pattern. Look where you will, inside the crumbling empires of France and England, or in those countries that were formerly semi-colonial — Egypt, China, Persia. It is the same war that is being waged, and the Welsh patriot stands hand in hand with resurgent Humanity the whole world over. In so far as he is nationally minded the Welshman today is one with the majority of the world's

population. In so far as he is anti-national, he is a museum piece, with Kipling and Colonel Blimp for company.

"Because we are nationally minded, and because our nation is temporarily incorporated in an alien empire, we feel a special responsibility to other countries in a similar position. We have given concrete help to the African leader Jomo Kenyatta, and have always been ready with encouragement and publicity for other struggling communities. In this number, for instance, we devote an article to the little-known case of Cyprus. Can as much be said for our enemies in Wales, for all their hypocritical protestations of 'world brotherhood'.

"Because we are nationally-minded, we come very near to something like Christian charity in our attitude to England — a country that most of us know and like and can even respect. After all, to have fought against the Welsh for many centuries is no mean feat, even if they never got very far until quite recently. England itself is equally the victim of a devouring imperialism which has undermined all her best traditions and delivered her ordinary people into the twilight of almost perpetual Toryism.

"To Wales, England has spoken not with the voice of Milton and Keats, but of Churchill and Mond.

"We may be excused if our criticisms are occasionally a little personal. Because we are nationally-minded we believe that our neighbouring communities must go their different ways to the benefit of both. Some elements in both countries fear that the Welsh Republican Movement wields the assassin's dagger. But in reality it is the surgeon's knife."

Noteworthy too, is the appearance again in this issue of work from the pen of Oxford exile, Ifor Huws Wilks, which was to be the first of a series written by him for the paper. 'REVOLT' is its graphic title over its graphic beginning:

"They shall be drawn on a hurdle to the place of execution, hanged until they are dead, their heads severed from their bodies, and the body of each shall be divided into four quarters which shall be placed at the disposal of Her Majesty" — Sir Nicholas Tindal, Lord Chief Justice of England.

"On the 16th of January, 1840, in a Monmouth heavily garrisoned with English troops, this barbarous sentence was passed (though ultimately commuted to transportation for life) upon three Welshmen, Zephania Williams of Blaina, William Jones of Pontypool, and John Frost of Newport. Under a statute of 1352 they had been found guilty of high treason by levying war against the English Queen. Some twenty of their fellow rebels had already been killed in the street fighting in Newport, and about fifty wounded. In the long series of trials that followed the rebellion, others were sentenced to varying terms of transportation, whilst by the end of 1840 the jails of South Wales held some 75 political prisoners who had taken part. As late as mid-1841 a Brynmawr rebel received seven years transportation.

"The period of the trials was marked by activity on the part both of the English troops and of such rebel leaders as had escaped identification. For even after the rebel failure to occupy Newport town on November 4th 1839, the mining valleys remained under rebel control. On the hills drilling and target practice continued unabated, and it was only as more and more troops were drafted into South Wales that the valleys, one by one, were brought back under English control. Even six weeks after the attack on Newport the English military commander there reported to the London Home Office that 'The Mayor is in great alarm and has, he says, the best information that there is to be a general rising'.

"But no fresh rising did occur. The rebels having lost the initial advantage of surprise, quietly hid their arms and in small groups drifted back to the pits and the ironworks. Subsequent events, however, showed that the Welsh workers were still strong in the spirit of resistance. The Scotch Cattle, an underground terrorist centred on Abersychan, renewed its activities. Powder stores were raided and explosives carried off. In 1843 the workers of Merthyr boasted of having 6,000 stands of arms ready for use. Yet a few years later a certain Edmund Jones, addressing the same Merthyr workers, was to set before them the example of Owain Glyndŵr's struggle against English oppression in the 15th century, and ask, tauntingly, if the Welsh of the 19th century were going to prove themselves, in comparison, cowards. Perhaps the taunt was unjust; certainly there was to be no further general rising in Wales for the remainder of the 19th century; but the creation of a militant trade union and socialist movement in Wales during that time showed that the old fires had not died out.

"Such was the aftermath of the Welsh Rebellion of 1839. Political observers at the time had little doubt about its magnitude. *The Western Vindicator*, an English Chartist paper sympathetic to the rebels, contained an account unequivocally headed 'Revolution in Wales'. And the London *Times*, traditionally hostile to Wales, despite itself, paid grudging tribute to the rebels, admitting that 'this long-planned insurrection, deeply organised, managed with a secrecy truly amazing, was defeated only by concurrent acts of Providence'. Nor was the English government itself disposed to minimize the seriousness and extent of the rebellion. At the very first trial, fourteen Welshmen whose identity had already been established, together with, so the indictment read, 'other false traitors to the number of two thousand and more', were arraigned for levying war against the Queen by marching in battle array, seizing arms, firing upon the magistrates and upon the Queen's troops and such other acts. Truly had the name of 'traitor' become an honourable one in Wales!

"But if contemporaries had little doubt of the extent of the rebellion, subsequent generations of historians, with an anti-Welsh and anti-working class bias, attempted to quietly relegate the rebellion to an insignificant place in the history of the struggles of the Welsh people. Thus an insurrection by which the Welsh workers hoped to seize power throughout South Wales, and set up their own polity, becomes distorted, in the history books, into a mere 'Newport riot' — as if a handful of drunkards had smashed a shop window. In like manner, English historians attempted to minimize the importance of the Irish Rebellion of 1798 — a rebellion which bore many similarities to the later Welsh one, and which sprang, like it, from the intolerable burdens imposed upon a people by an essentially alien administration."

These quotes from Aneurin Bevan as given in the paper are also worthy of note:

1. "Speaking in the House of Commons on Welsh Affairs, Mr Aneurin Bevan recently proclaimed: 'Although those of us who have been brought up in Monmouthshire and Glamorganshire are not Welsh-speaking, Welsh-writing Welshmen, nevertheless we are all aware of the fact that there exists in Wales a culture which is unique in the world. It is a special attitude towards mental things which one does not find anywhere else. *We are not prepared to see it die.*' "
2. "In the modern world imperialism is in conflict with nationalism, and nationalism is winning all the time."
3. "It is rather hard to see water gushing from Wales into England and Wales being left dry."

From an article by Dr D.J. Davies, Gilwern, entitled 'Welsh Labour Ideals', the following excerpt especially demands attention:

"Something is obviously wrong in the way English Labour is treading. Indeed, the relief with which *Time and Tide* and such imperialist papers exulted after 1945 because the Labour government's policy was identical with that of Tory governments, an illustration of the oneness of English ideals, should have made the Socialists uneasy. Keir Hardie certainly must have turned in his grave. For the Tory is an avowed imperialist, not overburdened with scruples in his dealings with other nations, his one aim being to exploit and subordinate them for England's benefit. 'Scratch an Englishman and find an imperialist' it is said, and the Labour Party has bought success in England by accepting the imperialism of England. Indeed, so thoroughly English (and imperialist) has the party become that even some Welsh MPs now think like Englishmen and react to the question of a Parliament for Wales, their own country (an issue between England and another nation), as an English Tory would do.

"There is only one honourable course before Welsh Socialists. Let us not be fooled by those who try to treat Socialism and Welsh patriotism as mutually antagonistic forces. We must cut adrift from English imperialists whether called Conservatives or Labour, and maintain the idealistic Socialism that first captured Welsh allegiance, that abhorred the exploitation of nation by nation as much as the exploitation of men by men. Let the English Labour Party continue to uphold the bloodstained imperialism of England if it will. We call upon Welsh Socialists to keep their basic principles — to the infinitely nobler aim of securing the welfare of ordinary Welsh men and women in a Free Wales."

In his article headed 'Welsh Democracy versus English Extremism' Cliff Bere was primarily concerned with English insistence on maintaining 'great power' status even if it meant increasing her already overflowing population (Labour Home Secretary Herbert Morrison had had the figure of 70 millions in mind). The final paragraph reads:

"We in Wales who have lived or died according to the dictates of English national policy, have today two roads before us.

"One leads on, as hitherto, under the shadow and domination of England to her future, uncertain and dark with the threat of social and economic chaos. The other is the road to national independence. It is only as a free nation that we shall have the opportunity of building a sane economic order to make Wales self-reliant to face the future, and the hope of maintaining democracy against the onset of political extremes in England."

Ac yn olaf, ond dichon nid y lleiaf yn ei arwyddocâd i ddyfodol Cymru hunan-lywodraethol yw'r cyfraniad hwn dan enw 'Alesandr' (I.O. Ellis, Rhuthun) ar bwnc 'Rheilffyrdd Cymru'. ('Syniadau unigolyn yw'r isod, nid polisi MGC') yw ei ragair cwrtais ei hun o flaen ei ysgrif:

"*Cafwyd erthyglau rhagorol ar gyflwr enbyd cysylltiadau mewnol Cymru yn y ddau rifyn diwethaf o'r* Gweriniaethwr. *Ac o edrych ar y map fe wêl yr hurtaf na ellir mynd o Wrecsam i Gaerdydd heb fynd trwy Loegr; yn wir, mae'r rhan fwyaf o'r daith trwy siroedd Amwythig a Henffordd. Os yw rhywun am aros ar dir Cymru rhaid iddo fynd trwy Gorwen, Dolgellau, Aberdyfi, Machynlleth, Moat Lane a Thalybont. Byddir yn siwr o gyrraedd Caerdydd, ond pa bryd?*

"*Ofnadwy iawn. Ond pa beth allai Gweriniaeth Gymreig ei wneud i wella pethau? Mentraf osod cynllun gerbron darllenwyr y papur hwn: adeiladu ffordd haearn newydd sbon o'r Waun i Gyffordd Moat Lane. Byddai'n ceincio oddi wrth ffordd Wrecsam-Amwythig i fyny Dyffryn Ceiriog hyd at Lanarmon D.C., twnel, ac ar draws Dyffryn Tanad, twnel arall i ddod allan ger Llanfyllin; yna i fyny Nant Alan, twnel i Ddyffryn Efyrnwy, yna i fyny Dyffryn Banw i Lanfair Caer Einion, twnel i Fanafon, ac ymlaen wedyn i Moat Lane. Byddai'n rhaid dyblu a moderneiddio'r ffordd o Moat Lane ymlaen drwy Lanidloes, Talybont, Merthyr a Pontypridd i Gaerdydd.*

"*Mae'n wir y byddai cost y cynllun yn fawr, ond byddai nwyddau a theithwyr yn cael eu cludo ar y ffordd newydd ynglŷn â busnes y Brifddinas. Byddai cynnyrch diwydiannol Wrecsam yn cael ei allforio drwy Gaerdydd, a dygid glo ardal Wrecsam a'r Deheudir i'r Canolbarth drwy'r cysylltiad effeithiol hwn. Âi defaid, eidion a llefrith y Gogledd a'r Canolbarth i'r De, a deuai drwy Gaerdydd fewnforion bwydydd, coed tramor, mwynau a nwyddau masnachol o bob math.*

"*Ni byddai'r twneli a grybwyllwyd yn rhai hirion. Ni byddai'r hwyaf ond bedair milltir o hyd, bach iawn o'i gymharu â'r Yswistir. O Wrecsam gellid adeiladu hefyd ffordd haearn i gysylltu â ffordd Caer-Caergybi. Nid y rheilffyrdd yn unig a gai fudd o'r cynllun hwn. Deuai ffyrdd i geir modur yn naturiol yn ei sgil, a gellid datblygu ffyrdd i gysylltu De a Gogledd, Abertawe ac Abergele, Corwen a Chaerau, gan uno a chyfoethogi'r genedl ar yr un pryd wrth ei gwasanaethu.*"

★ ★ ★

Republican activities on the streets of the Valley towns were now mainly concerned with the sale of the Republican paper. But when a gathering of three or four activists was able to be arranged, usually on a Saturday, street corner meetings were still held, with much of the old enthusiasm and enjoyable challenge.

However, if activities on the streets no longer had the frequency and urgency of previous years, *The Welsh Republican* itself, under the editorship of Harri

Webb, was still going from strength to strength in quality and reputation.

The April-May 1954 issue has a little item on the front page which can be read almost as a portent of the disaster to befall not much more than a decade into the future in the Merthyr Valley. 'Welsh Children Cheated', it is headed.

> "In the narrow valleys the only playground is often the street. English capitalists piled up great tips of colliery waste that could have been spread out and put to social uses. Crippled by years of depression, held up by war and shortages, our Local Authorities still strove to make some use of the tips. In the Garw, for instance, they started to make a playing-field. The Ministry of Education made a grant. Then came the Tory 'Education' policy, and the economy cuts. The grant for the Garw project was withdrawn. The work is at a standstill. And the children of the Garw and scores of such communities in Wales are left with only the streets to play in.
>
> "Carry on Miss Horsborough, Tory 'Minister of Education' — Don't you feel like an admiral of the Swiss Navy sometimes? Carry on, my lords and gentlemen, Tory MPs of the future on the fine playing-fields of the public schools. Carry on, your Majesty, on your yacht that cost just a bit too much. You may stop us building our recreation grounds, but you are building up something else in Wales. You will be hearing from the children of the narrow valleys!"

Neges ddarogan o fath hefyd sydd yn llith fach Huw Davies, 'Dinasyddiaeth', ond, y tro hwn, wrth ragweld gobaith o ddoethineb, yn hytrach na thrychineb, yn dod yn y dyfodol i fendithio'r genedl.

> " . . . *Canys mewn ysbryd hael o gyd-ddeall, ac ar seiliau eang o ran hil ac iaith, yr adeiledir Cymru Fydd. Gosodwn nod y bydd raid wrth amser i'w gyrraedd: gwlad rydd lle y bydd y Gymraeg eto'n iaith y mwyafrif. Dyry Oes Newydd Cymru gyfle Cymreictod llawn i bob dinesydd. Bydd dyletswydd yn gyfartal â'r hawl. Braint Cymry Cymraeg yw cyflwyno'r etifeddiaeth genedlaethol. Rhyddhad y Cymro di-Gymraeg fydd anghofio'i golled a gweithio dros well byd i'w blant. Boed croeso hefyd i'r Sais a ddaw i mewn i'w ddinasyddiaeth Gymraeg â pharch ac ewyllys da. Unir yr elfennau gwahanol hyn gan genedligrwydd Cymreig cryf a goleuedig ar gyfer ymdrechion yr oes bresennol a champweithiau'r oesau a ddêl."*

And indeed, it is the brief, bright items throughout this issue which seem to make it an irresistible duty to have to quote as many as possible of them here, to the exclusion of almost everything else.

> "Eisteddfoddity! — We congratulate the Council of the National Eisteddfod on their continued stand for Welsh as the only appropriate

language for our People's Festival. Only suburban snobs and Kemsley-ite illiterates will carp at this enlightened decision."

"*Mau Mau in Norfolk — You can never tell.* There was once a native tribe which became incorporated in a world-wide, civilized Empire. But the unimaginative policy of the central government and the brutality of imperial officials on the spot caused the tribe to revolt. Under a gifted leader they fought a victorious campaign and took revenge for their exploitation. Their methods were primitive, bloody and terrible. The imperial retaliation was no less terrible. Oddly enough none of this happened in Africa, but in Britain. The tribal leader's name was Boadicea and she has been regarded as a heroine ever since. There is even a statue of her in bronze just outside the Parliament of Westminster, where you have only got to mention Mau-Mau to raise gasps of horror!"

"*Controversy Corner — Are Missions Necessary?* Wales has always been noted for missionaries. There was Gweirydd ap Rhys, for instance, who was rescued from the cooking pot by a beautiful young African chieftainess, and nearly stayed on to rule the tribe . . . But that was before the great awakening in Africa and Asia. Today the voices of Dr Malan and Captain Griffiths speak louder in Africa than the voices of men like Albert Schweitzer. When the Europeans are so backward at applying the doctrines of Christianity, we cannot expect the Africans and Asians to be very enthusiastic converts. Today indeed, Christian missions are looked at askance as tools of Western imperialism. 'Western civilization' cannot export both the Hydrogen bomb and the Sermon on the Mount — which was preached in Asia in the first place, anyway.

"Is it not time for Wales to cease pouring away all the spiritual and national resources that go to the Mission Field? Is not our own nation bound and bleeding on the altars of Mammon and Moloch — twin deities of the English Vampire State. Where will our idealistic and energetic spirits most appropriately labour for justice and righteousness between man and man — on the Khasai Hills or the Cambrian Mountains?"

"*THE HEROES — What they don't allow to be taught in Welsh schools.* In this space for many numbers past, we have been running a feature which has outstripped all others in popularity to judge by the volume of favourable comments we have received: Our series spotlighting the Risings, Strikes, Revolts and Agitations which make up the Welsh Fighting Century. We could have continued this series for many numbers to come, but we thought you might appreciate a slightly different presentation. So we are going over this rich field again, with the emphasis on the personalities rather than on the broad historic sweep of events. And what personalities! Only Wales could produce them: stainless young martyrs like Dic Penderyn and George Shell; strange mixtures of prophet and showman like Iolo Morgannwg and William Price; Ieuan Gwynedd, the young preacher who burnt himself out in a flame of love for Wales and her people; Emrys ap Iwan, master of satire and straight thinking; enigmatic figures lurking in the torchlight on the edge of rebellion, like Lewis the Huntsman, or striding masterfully in its midst like John Frost, Mayor of Newport; Rebecca, the great Unknown, mysterious in the trappings of Celtic myth among the hedge-poets, bruisers and lads of the village who swept English rule out of West Wales — and in stern contrast, the sober daylight figures of the organisers and militant workers' leaders who struck and struck again at the owners and masters and magistrates, all the embattled Powers of Darkness with an invincible Empire at their backs.

"These are the people you will read about in *The Welsh Republican*. These are the people who will one day be held up for admiration in the schools of Wales instead of foreign crooks like Marlborough and Drake. Until that day comes we need your help. This is your paper, it serves the Welsh people. It is not an imperialist poison-sheet nor a literary review. We welcome any items or articles you like to send us (500 words maximum), any exposure of the abuses and shortcomings of English rule, anything that will contribute to the informed, combative spirit of National Militancy. Also, we need your material help, your contributions, donations, subscriptions (see advt. on this page). Above all, Wales needs your services. You seem to have liked reading about the great deeds of the past — there is a future, too, beginning now.

YOU ARE NEEDED FOR IT!

But it is with a sad note of farewell to a man we were proud to have known that the items of this issue have to end:

OBITUARY

William Henry Lloyd
Stow Hill, Newport, Mon.
5th December, 1953
A Tribute

"Death with a swift, unexpected blow has removed from our midst at the age of 47 a great-hearted Welshman and Patriot. It is a loss that will not soon be got over. From his early years William Lloyd devoted himself with unflagging energy to the cause of the working-people of these islands. During his period of exile over the border, he founded in the erstwhile Tory preserve of Didcot a branch of the English Labour party and he was asked to run for mayor.

But in recent years it was the affairs and needs of his own country to which he gave his attention and allegiance. Never far from his thoughts or his conversation was the story of how his family, two generations ago, were driven, after heroic resistance, from their homestead in the Elan Valley and left to wander homeless in the countryside, so that Birmingham might have a free hand to impound the waters of their native valley for its own use.

"Perhaps it was this family memory that helped to make him so earnest a spokesman, so ready with help for the underdog and the destitute. In the Hungry Thirties he led the hunger marches from Newport to London, he campaigned on the street corners of Newport, and no-one who came to his door in need of food or help was turned away.

"Last Autumn he travelled overnight to Southampton to see his 18 year old son embark for abroad with the 1st Battalion Welsh Guards. In the midst of that suffocating jingoistic atmosphere (contributed to by the failure or refusal of the quayside band to play the Welsh tunes the soldiers were calling for) it was the Red Dragon flag raised on the quayside by William Lloyd which drew the one full-throated cheer.

"And now he has handed over that banner into the keeping of others. He will not be forgotten by his fellow-members of the Welsh Republican Movement. The one memorial worthy of him will be our victory in the fight for Welsh Independence in which he was so glad to join."

★ ★ ★

At the end of June 1954 Pedr Lewis was released from Stoke-on-Trent prison where he had been since May of the previous year. A formal 'Welcome home' had been arranged for him at an Abertawe hotel, when an appreciable sum of money, collected mainly via the Assistance Fund of the WRM, was presented to him, and which he referred to in the course of a stimulating address as his 'National Insurance'.

Amongst the many well-wishers, Republicans and others, at the gathering was one who made himself prominent in the welcoming celebrations as a self-declared fervent supporter of the Republican cause. The fact that he was hitherto unknown to any of those present had tended to pass unnoticed in the general atmosphere of rejoicing. Unknown, that is, except to one young woman supporter who had eventually turned up at the gathering and who had been employed at one time in relation to police matters. She was able to identify him as a man who, if not on police staff himself, was directly involved and employed in police affairs. Further proof of this emerged very soon after.

This little story, of course quite unsurprising in itself, demonstrates so very clearly once again how the long arm of the law of the English State is ever poised to reach out to any lengths, unrelaxing, unrelenting where there is any suggestion of political threat perceived.

Chapter 20

The Welsh Republican — Y Gweriniaethwr was now probably the most effective written medium of propaganda in the Nationalist cause. In the cogency and incisiveness, the invigorating readability of its message it had never been excelled. The steady increase in its list of subscribers lent testimony to that. And now, looking back over the long years one has to recognize that the controlling editorial hand of Wizard Webb ensconced in the homely, comparatively peaceful confines of his library in Dowlais must in large part take the credit for this.

It was undoubtedly the success of its paper which helped the Welsh Republican Movement to reconcile itself to the change of activities enforced by circumstances upon it. Perhaps the front page article of the June-July 1954 issue can be read as a pointer again to the direction in which things were moving. Over its heading 'Wales and the Miners — a Shake-up for the Old Gang', it ran:

> "Welsh Home Rule marches on — This Summer it has secured a bridgehead of incalculable strategic importance. The issue of a 'Parliament for Wales' has been debated in the Welsh Miners Conference at Porthcawl. After earnest and lengthy debate, the idea was turned down. But this is no reflection on the patriotism of the miners. Rather it is tribute to their integrity. For the proposals they were called upon to discuss were shaky in the extreme.
>
> "The shortcomings of the Parliament for Wales Campaign have been pointed out before now in *The Welsh Republican*, and its particular inadequacy from the colliers' point of view is discussed in detail by our Industrial Correspondent on page four of this number.
>
> "It was a severe setback to the enemies of Wales that a national issue ever even reached the Miners Conference. *Reactionary elements strained every nerve to keep Welsh Self-Government off the Agenda. But the miners insisted on discussing it.*
>
> "What a contrast to the days when the only countries that it was polite to mention in these meetings were China, Abyssinia, Spain and other

such conveniently remote victims of aggression. How much cleaner the atmosphere is now. How bright the horizon!

"Although most of the delegates voted against the idea, the number in favour was far from negligible, and even more significant was the still larger proportion of those who abstained. Many of them did not wish to vote against such old-timers as Dai Grenfell and Jim Griffiths.

"For these were the big guns who were sent down especially to speak against Wales, *and for no other purpose*. If you weren't there you may have heard the recorded extracts of the speeches made in this debate, and the Welsh Broadcasting Authorities deserve our thanks for giving the whole nation the chance of comparing the speakers on both sides, for in their voices lay the whole contrast, the whole crux of this matter: on the one, the successful, tired old men who discourage new ideas, whose minds were formed in a by-gone age, their voices by now keyed to the decorous murmurs of the 'Best Club in Europe'. In ringing contrast, the voices of Cyril Parry, Dick Beamish, Glyn Phillips and their supporters — these men are still at the coalface, in the midst of the practical day-to-day problems of Welsh industry, their ears attuned to the vibration of coal-cutter and the clatter of conveyor belt — and the harsh, dry cough of the 'dust' victim. *They* are the voice of Wales. In these miners leaders of the future speaks the future of our nation.

"To the short-sighted, self-interested and plain dumb who oppose National Independence we commend the words of *John Penry*, a young man who went to the gallows for Wales when our country lay under the renegade heel of the bloody Tudors. To the complacent and neglectful social leaders of his day he addressed these vividly topical words:

" 'I know you for the most part to be silly men — poor souls that make a means to live in the world. What should I say unto you, who may say of yourselves as did the foolish prophets: "Surely the people may ask counsel as well of their thresholds, or desire their staffs to teach them knowledge as come unto you for instruction. Give over your places! Better it were to live poorly here for a time than to be undone for ever." ' "

The second in the series of Studies of the Rebellion of 1839 by Ifor Huws Wilks is presented in this issue under the title 'A Noble Cause. No. 2 The Background of a Rebellion'. The first few chapters are given here:

" 'We are the descendants of valiant Welshmen, and we must be worthy of the traditions which they have passed on to us. It is far better that we should die fighting for freedom than live as slaves of greed and opulence. Today we are fighting for something more than our freedom — for that of our children and the children of our children'. William Price, Surgeon, of Merthyr.

" 'Dear Parents, — I hope this will find you well, as I am myself at present. I shall this night be engaged in a struggle for freedom, and should it please God to spare me, I shall see you soon; but if not, grieve not for me. I shall fall in a noble cause. My tools are at Mr Cecil's, and likewise my clothes. Yours truly, George Shell.'

"Dr William Price addressed the Merthyr workers a few days before the Rebellion of 1839, and shortly, disguised as a woman, with £100 offered for his capture by a badly shaken English government, he was to make good his escape to Paris. George Shell of Pontypool wrote to his parents a few hours before the rebel march on Newport, and within the day lay dead in the street fighting. Price of the rebel leadership, Shell of the rank-and-file, both alike typified the spirit that was abroad in South Wales.

"The Welsh Rebellion of 1839 was the major Welsh Rising of the century. But it took place against the whole backcloth of Welsh history. Three centuries earlier an English parliament had passed the so-called Act of Union of 1536, a remarkable piece of legal chicanery expressly designed to undermine all Welsh political, legal and social institutions, the Welsh language included, and so reduce Wales to an indistinguishable part of the English realm. This genocidal policy failed; Wales retained its identity. But it was a divided Wales, wherein two hostile nations confronted each other, and still did so in the 19th century. The one was alien, a society of the anglicized gentry, of the capitalist coal and iron-masters, of the reactionary Church of England. It was a society deriving its power, authority and culture from England, a society exercising all the functions of English rule in Wales. But it was a society whose very existence in Wales was shown, time and time again throughout the 19th century, to possess no other basis than the sabres and muskets of England's soldiery.

"Distinct from this alien society was the Welsh nation proper — no racial entity, but a vigorous and ancient community which absorbed all immigrants so that they became as Welsh as the Welsh themselves. It was a community deprived of its own institutions, its language scorned, its traditional democracy denied effective outlet. Yet in this community behind the barriers of language, religion and folk memories, the spirit of Wales remained inviolable and indestructible. The common people of Wales cherished their past, and found in it hope for the future. And it was these people who, in the South Wales of 1839, were to attempt to wrest the instruments of government out of the alien hands. *The Welsh Rebellion of 1839 was an answer to the economic distress, social injustice, and political frustration consequent upon English rule in Wales."*

★ ★ ★

In the enthusiasm and rejoicing of 'Empire's End', celebrating the end of French colonial rule in Indo-China, there is as yet no presentiment of the infinitely more bloody sequel to that dark chapter of imperial history — and of the insuperable heroism that was to endure throughout and come through into an immortal victory.

"Of all the nauseating stunts that the English tripe press has tried to thrust down the throats of the Welsh people, the attempt to invest French rule in Indo-China with the prestige of 'Western Civilization' has been the most impertinent — and the biggest flop.

"The French Empire, like the English Empire, is on the way out. In Indo-China French rule was responsible for mass degredation and misery on a terrible scale. One of the chief sources of revenue to the glorious French Empire was a liquor tax. The Indo-Chinese, like many Eastern races, do not drink much. So liquor was forced on village headmen and its consumption made practically compulsory. The effects of tolerated mass-drunkenness on a simple, abstemious people living near the poverty line may be easily imagined. This deliberate barbarization of an ancient society is characteristic of the French Empire whose symbols — from Brittany to Cambodia — are the Barracks and the Brothel.

"The victory of General Giap at Dien Bien Phu is saluted by Welsh Republicans and patriots everywhere as a people's victory. We have no tears to spare for the gang of feudal playboys, mercenary adventurers and ex-Nazi thugs whose fate sent the English press into hysterics and made the culture-loving French people kick the Russian Ballet out of Paris. All along the line, from Indo-China in the throes of a liberating war, Tunisia with its bloody commotions, Algeria where the brutality of French troops will be an indelible memory, Morocco with its Nationalist Sultan in exile, to our own Celtic Brittany, the French are in a panic. They have at last been obliged to let the Breton patriot Andre Geoffroy out of jail where he lay for years under sentence of death merely for being a patriot. So the ends of the Earth are met together to rejoice in freedom. To Giap of Viet Minh, to

Geoffroy of Brittany, our hearts and hands go out in fellowship. *Sic semper tyrannis"*

Writing on 'A Great Patriot — Casement of Ireland' a contributor, 'Deeside', ends his article with this excerpt from Casement's noble address from the dock when he was sentenced to death:

"Ireland has outlived all the failure of her hopes, and yet she still hopes. For if English authority be omnipotent, Irish hope exceeds the dimension of that power, excels the authority, and renews with each generation the claims of the last. The cause that begets this indomitable persistency, the faculty of preserving through centuries of misery the remembrance of lost liberty, this surely is the noblest cause men ever strove for, ever lived for, ever died for. If this is the cause I stand here today indicted for, and convicted of sustaining, then I stand in a goodly company and a right noble succession."

Yes indeed — to all those of us in Cymru with any measure of realistic patriotic pride and self-respect in us — again and again Casement's words must surely strike home.

★ ★ ★

In June 1954 Cliff Bere was appointed organizer for South-East Wales in the Parliament for Wales Campaign. Gwynfor Evans, President of Plaid Cymru then and for many years after, was a member of the joint-party Campaign Committee making the appointment, and although it was, and still remains, surmise on his part, the appointee thought it very probable that it was through the good offices, as the saying goes, of Gwynfor Evans that this appointment came to be made.

As Bere was very much identified with the Republicans, that appointment signified that that generation of the Welsh Republican Movement's more actionist policies would almost inevitably have to end. Soon the duties of the Campaign came to demand almost every waking minute of the newly appointed organizer's time. To add to the pressure of work now falling upon him, his wife was called away to tend to her ailing mother, and by the end of June, taking her two little sons with her, had left for Y Bala to be at her mother's side in her terminal illness.

From the now very empty and echoing spaces of the four-bedroomed house and shop premises in Heol Gilfach, Bargoed, the South-East organizer pursued his mission through the same familiar Valley towns as before, its message of patriotism different now only in degree. But now, of course, with the help in those towns of other willing eager hands.

There was a peak of activity in the Autumn involving the organization of five

Campaign meetings addressed by Megan Lloyd George together with other very able speakers — in Maesteg on the Wednesday, Pontypridd and Treorci on the Thursday, and Glyn Ebwy (*Ebbw Vale*) and Abertyleri on the Friday, all of which were — undoubtedly largely due to the magnetism of the Lloyd George name — immensely successful in attracting great and overflowing attendances in each of the five venues.

Some time before this, Cliff Bere had been able to secure a contract for the sale of 104, Heol Gilfach. By mischance, or possibly misjudgment on his part, the time and day for handing over the premises to the new owner arrived in the very midst of the work of organizing the above meetings. Bere woke on the morning of that day faced with the task of preparing and packing by himself the entire contents of the house (the shop was already empty) ready for collection by 3 pm that day for storage at the Pickford depot in Caerdydd. Due to the pressure of Campaign commitments he had been unable to find a spare moment before this to put his hand to that work of preparation. Even the stair-carpet rod-holders awaited to be unscrewed!

Suffice to say that the memory of that day is seared on the mind of one Republican to the end of his days. After the removal men had gone, the dusty house was swept clean, its immense accumulation of unwanted paper-work having to be left as a tidy enough mountain in the backyard. Shortly before 7 pm he was able to deliver the house keys to the new owner, a Mr Jarman living not many doors away in Heol Gilfach, before turning to force his weary steps towards the — oh so distant! — railway station and the bliss of sitting down in the train to Caerdydd.

No. 104, Heol Gilfach was sold for £700, the amount necessary to repay the mortgage on the premises. So ended the story of 'Siop Lyfrau a Llyfrgell Bargoed Bookshop and Library' and its brief rôle in the history of the Republican Movement in Cymru.

* * *

Under the very able and dedicated management of Mr Elwyn Roberts, the General Organizer of the Parliament for Wales Campaign, together with the efforts of his assistant organizers in the South and North, and most important all, the efforts of the many who voluntarily gave their time and energy unsparingly to carry the Campaign Petition forms from door to door, a total of nearly a quarter of a million signatures was eventually achieved. It is generally considered that it was as a result of this impressive, unmistakeable expression of opinion that under a Labour Government in October 1964 the Office of Secretary of State for Wales first came into being.

And there may be a touch of irony about the fact that it was from the garage business in Ystradmynach from which he had been so summarily dismissed in

1952 that the South-East organizer, after returning to Caerdydd, purchased for £50 an old but eminently serviceable motor-car (vintage, Jowett, 1934) which did indeed give invaluable and uncomplaining service in the work of the Campaign.

Chapter 21

The Welsh Republican — Y Gweriniaethwr had for some time now been published from the address rented from Mr W. Charles Owen at 144b, City Road, Caerdydd. The following bold insert from the August-September 1954 issue gives an indication of the success the paper was having and the feeling of confidence behind its promotion.

TO ALL OUR READERS
Would you like to see
THE WELSH REPUBLICAN
Coming out twice as often as it does now?
You can help to bring that day nearer.
We are within striking distance of our target:
**A MONTHLY PAPER VINDICATING
WELSH RIGHTS, CHALLENGING THE INJUSTICES
AND EXPOSING THE INEFFICIENCIES OF
ALIEN RULE**
If you have liked reading The Welsh Republican
over the past few years,
If you want to do something, however small, in the struggle,
If you love Wales
YOU WILL HELP NOW!
Send a gift of money to the:
Managing Editor, WELSH REPUBLICAN
144b, City Road, Cardiff
All contributions will be gratefully acknowledged.

This issue saw the third of Ifor Huws Wilks' studies in the 1839 Rebellion. 'Ripe to Rebel' was the sub-heading over its second chapter:

> "It was probably late in 1839 that the activity began which was to finally produce the bid for power of 1839. In a matter of months by some tremendous release of energy the comparatively small body known as the Scotch Cattle must have been transformed into an organization reaching into every town or village throughout South

Wales. By March 1839 the Mayor of Newport was already reporting to the Home Office in London that arms were being distributed in South Wales, and that an insurrection might be expected unless checked in time. In April the landowners and coal-and iron-masters of Monmouthshire, perturbed by the growing threat to their security, met near Newport and, pledging loyalty to the English Queen, sponsored their own defence force to combat the rising which they were expecting daily. Doubtless the Welsh workers applied the logic of this to their own case: if the rich were justified in arming in defence of their interests, then so too were the 'gwerin'. And arm they did! Something like a panic gripped the authorities. By May 1839 the Mayor of Swansea was negotiating with the Home Office for troops and a sloop-of-war with marines to be stationed in the town. By June the Lord Lieutenant of Glamorgan informed London that the people were 'ripe to rebel!', and requested that troops should be posted to strategic points throughout South Wales. '*The working people are constantly practising firing at targets*', reported the Glamorgan magistrates. And as the year progressed such reports became ever more frequent, ever more frantic.

"Various accounts give glimpses of what was happening in those Welsh valleys where men worked in the pits and foundries and shops by day, and drilled on the hills by night. We learn, for instance, that agents were commissioned by the rebels to buy up arms, and, on the mountainsides, smithies were established where pikes, bullets, helmets and even cannon were manufactured. A recruiting system was introduced which probably derived from that used in the Irish Rebellion of 1798, for there are similarities between the two, *and some evidence suggests that Irish rebels, who had escaped from Ireland and were perhaps amongst the gangs of Irish labourers employed on the construction of the Welsh docks and railways, were not averse to giving their Welsh counterparts the benefit of their experience*. Thus we find the Welsh rebels recruited into Sections of ten men, each with a Captain who alone was in touch with other Sections. Five such Sections probably constituted a Group, three Groups a Company, and three Companies a Brigade. A Brigade would thus contain about 450 men and perhaps 50 Officers. In any one district it would appear that all the Brigades were controlled by what was called the Lodge — possibly an administrative rather than a fighting formation. The Abersychan Lodge may have been typical. It was apparently led by a soldier of 25 years experience who had fought at Waterloo. He claimed to have 1600 men under him (i.e. 3 Brigades), 1200 of whom were trained in the use of weapons, and the remainder actively under training. A number of such Lodges as this one were probably responsible to a Head Committee. We hear of one such Committee at Cyfarthfa, 'who are very particular in excluding common members from their deliberations'.

"*With this widespread organization at their disposal, sometime in mid-1839 the Head Committees, as we shall see, produced a carefully worked out plan designed to wrest power in South Wales permanently from the hands of the alien English administration.*"

This issue also saw the welcome return of Ithel Davies to its pages. His contribution begins:

"The Welsh Regional Council of Labour and the anti-Welsh Labour members have been greatly concerned at the growth of nationalist feeling in Wales. They were shaken at the vote of the Miners Conference which showed a healthy and vigorous minority opinion amongst the workers for their nation and her future."

After making telling mockery of anti-Welsh attitudes amongst Labour MPs and Union members in general, this great and steadfast Republican and Socialist ends with a more specific and richly deserved execration:

"The laurel must surely go to that other Welshman (sic) D.J. Williams, MP for Neath, who has the temerity to say that Socialism admits of no devolution such as is now proposed by the Campaign for a Welsh Parliament. *That is so only to the extent that true Socialism would demand not a Parliament for Wales such as is now proposed, but a full-blown status of political sovereignty. Socialists who do not demand that for every national community have betrayed every vestige of Socialist idealism and principle.*"

After a perceptive forward-looking article by Gwilym Prys Dafis under the title 'Rural Wales: The Way Ahead', there come two timely little items in the 'News Reel' column.

First: "A good Example. A young Swiss girl working as a domestic servant in England turns out to be the daughter of the President of the Swiss Republic, completing the practical side of her degree in Domestic Science. And nobody in Switzerland thought twice about it. What a healthy contrast to the vulgarity, frivolity and hysteria with which the activities of the young women of the English royal family are blazoned abroad! Which of these patterns of behaviour is more in accordance with the Welsh way of life?"

Then: "A Free Flag. The Irish naval vessel 'Macha' visited Aberystwyth this summer on a training cruise. And a very tiddly ship too, with the Tricolour of a free Republic flying from the ensign staff. We hope that this visit, from the efficient Armed Forces of the only free Celtic country, will not be the last. And we hope its significance was not lost on the traditionally sea-going Cardis — and all young Welshmen with the red blood of Morgan in their veins."

And last but by no means least in this issue is the movingly written 'Glorious Figures from our Past' for Dic Penderyn:

"After the French Revolution and the Welsh prophets of its doctrines of Liberty had brought a dawn of clear light to the mind of our country, the sky became reddened and murky with the flames and smoke of the Industrial Revolution. After the thinkers and writers came the workers' leaders, the men of action. You will not find their names in the New Dictionary of Welsh Biography — the lawyers and the preachers have not left much room. We know barely the names of the men who led the Merthyr risings of 1801 and 1811; of their life and character, hardly anything. Why, after all, should we? They were humble, ordinary men, who emerged once into the light of history only to sink again into the darkness of apparent failure. Our historians have still got a lot to do.

"But there is one shining example. Against the dark background of conspiracy and unrest, the figure of DICK PENDERYN stands out with vivid clarity: Richard Lewis, the boy from Pyle, who saved his friend from drowning in Aberavon Harbour. Dic Penderyn, the young married man who leapt out of the obscurity of a collier's life to lead the Merthyr Rising of 1831 to astounding success. Dic who lived in the memory of all who knew him, so clearly that even the little things about him were remembered until the time came to write them down: his good looks, his popularity, even his fondness for a pint. And now that cherished memory, that clear picture, belongs to the whole of Wales. His name is inscribed with those of Princes and Saints and Poets in the hearts of the nation. For at 22, Dic led and inspired the workers of Merthyr Tydfil and the whole Iron-belt of North Glamorgan in the rising that ambushed one English force, disarmed another, and drilled with captured arms to meet the enemy yet again. Taken prisoner while the issue was yet undecided, convicted on a trumped-up charge, Dic was publicly hanged at Cardiff Jail in a storm of thunder and lightning so terrible that many saw in it the protest of Heaven itself at this act of savagery. His funeral was turned into a triumphant procession of thousands, and the felon's grave at Aberavon is known and visited to this day. With such an example, the Welsh workers fought on, and can be relied upon to display the same characteristics that have so nearly brought success so often in the past. For the struggle goes on . . . YOU ARE NEEDED FOR IT!"

But the long list of 'Glorious Figures from our Past' is barely begun. The story of Shoni 'Sguborfawr, Twm Carnabwth, Dai'r Cantwr, Zephaniah Williams, Lewsyn yr Heliwr, George Shell, Lewis Humphreys — Bugler of Liberty, and of a dozen such again, are similarly, lovingly recorded in turn in successive copies of *Y Gweriniaethwr* up to the time of its last issue in April-May 1957. And some of them will be recorded in the final chapter of this work, together with much else of the best from the pages of the paper up to that closing issue.

★ ★ ★

But still for recording in this present chapter must be some of the invaluable contents of the October-November issue leading up to the end of the year 1954. In his editorial Harri Webb quotes from the speech of Aneurin Bevan addressing the National Committee of the Chinese People's Consultative Conference earlier that year:

" ' . . . The second respect in which we differ from you is that the struggles which you have waged are at the same time a struggle for national independence against imperialism. This has the effect of supercharging the social struggle with the emotions derived from national self-consciousness and the yearning for liberation. You are therefore possessed of an emotional dynamic which is not present with us'.

"Mr Bevan comes from the Tops of the Valleys. It is hard to believe that even in China he can have forgotten the difference between the exploitation of the English worker and the wholesale rape and ruin of that region where the epic desolation of Dowlais, the generation of despair that engulfed Blaina and Brynmawr seal the utter damnation before God and man of the Gentlemen of England.

"No national struggle against foreign imperialism indeed! No emotional dynamic! Mr Bevan has not only strayed into the very dead-end described in the first quotation above, he has undermined the whole 'raison d'être', the 'pace' and power of 'Bevanite' socialism. He has in effect disproved his own existence.

"This is not good enough. He, and the whole Labour Movement, must learn (the hard way if necessary) that only by fusing the ancient national aspirations of the Welsh people with their equally deep-rooted passion for social justice will any progress out of the present stagnation be possible."

And under the title 'Ballot — or Bullet? — Reformers and Radicals', the first three paragraphs of No. 4 in Ifor Wilks' series on the 1839 Rebellion pose the perennial question for which Freedom Movements have to find their own answer:

"In the 1830s the peoples of the nations of Europe were stirring; new revolutionary doctrines were whispered to the furthest corners of the continent. Soon 1848 was to become the Year of Revolutions; when scarcely a capital in Europe but heard the muskets rattle, saw the sabres flash. But first, for those that had ears to hear, a portent of this Year of Revolutions was to come from a small nation whose political development, like that of so many other European countries, had been arrested by a powerful neighbour. That small nation was Wales, where a degree of industrialisation as yet undreamed of in most of Europe had created a large wage-earning class receptive of new movements in a way that a conservative peasantry could never be. The portent was the Welsh Rebellion of 1839.

"The key to an understanding of the Welsh revolutionary movement of 1839 lies in that opposition which developed between middle-class reformers and working-class radicals — an opposition later to prove so universal a characteristic of other comparable European movements. The spirit of the reforming wing of the Welsh Movement was typified in its unchallenged leader, John Frost, a prosperous Newport Draper, Mayor of that town in 1836, and a magistrate. For many years a staunch advocate of national and municipal reform, Frost was to champion the cause of Chartism in South Wales and win for it a mass following. But for all that, Frost and the reformers remained essentially constitutionalists; by means of petitions, demonstrations, and parliamentary representation, they believed that the Charter would become law throughout England and Wales.

"But the outwardly 'united front' of the Welsh movement also contained a radical and republican wing which looked beyond the Charter to the dawn of a new era of liberty and justice.

" 'The points embodied in this Charter,' announced Dr William Price, 'are our immediate demands, but ultimately we shall demand more. Oppression, injustice and the grinding poverty which burdens our lives must be abolished for all times.' And the pages of '*Y Diwygiwr*' at the time testify that Socialism, which was everywhere inspiring European radicals with its message of fresh hope, did not lack its advocates in Wales. In line with the European revolutionary tradition, the Welsh radicals did not share the reformist faith in the English Parliament and constitution as an instrument of change. And bitter experience had convinced the Welsh workers that the bullet would speak louder in their case than the ballot. 'Remember Paris' became a familiar catch-phrase in those Welsh valleys where, behind the cover of orthodox political activity, an organization of trained and armed men was rapidly created . . . "

A letter of admiration for this series on the Rebellion of 1839 is well worth its inclusion here:

" *'Rwyf yn cael blas anghyffredin ar gyfres erthyglau I.H. Wilks yn* Y Gweriniaethwr; *mae'n beth go newydd yng Nghymru i gael darllen peth o'n hanes milwrol. Ac yn wir, mae'r gyfundrefn addysg Seisnig wedi gwneud llawer i ddifetha pob agwedd ar hanes milwrol Cymru. Ond dyma Gymro'n ymroi ati i gloddio am y manylion hyn; ni wn i ddim a ydyw'n sylweddoli hyn, ond mae o'n cryfhau cryn dipyn ar ein hysbryd cenedlaethol.*

"Bu'r hanesydd Tsiecaidd Palatsci yn cloddio yn yr un modd yn y ganrif ddiwethaf, a'r canlyniad i'r adfywiad oedd sefydlu Gweriniaeth Tsiecoslofacia yn 1918. Beth am Gymru? Mae hi'n wahanol, medd rhai. Tybed? Mae hi'n wlad arall mewn oes arall, ond a ellir dweud rhagor? Pan fydd dynion a chenhedloedd yn turio i'r gorffennol byddant yn gosod sylfeini yng ngorffennol eu cenedl (nid ar y gorffennol, cofier), ac y mae'r sylfeini dyfnion hynny'n eu cadw ar eu traed pan ddaw'r dydd i fynnu rhyddid.

"Sonnir yn yr erthygl 'Ripe to Rebel' am Bwyllgor yng Nghyfarthfa yn 'cadw materion milwrol o glyw a golwg aelodau cyffredin'. Dyna debygrwydd i'r Gwyddyl eto; 'roedd yr IRB enwog felly. Mae llawer wedi dweud pethau atgas am y polisi hwn, ond fe dalodd yn y pen draw pan dorrodd y Gwrthryfel allan yn 1916. 'Roedd byddin Lloegr yn Iwerddon yn gorffwys, a llawer o'r swyddogion ar egwyl; 'roedd Gwrthryfel y Pasg yn hollol annisgwyliadwy. Dymunaf gloi trwy ddiolch yn fawr iawn i'r awdur hwn am yr erthyglau ardderchog hyn ar hanes milwrol ein cenedl.

ALESANDAR"

The first and the last paragraphs of Ithel Davies' article under the title 'Rights of the Colonies' must suffice to sum up that which he states so clearly and well:

"The English Labour party has issued a policy for the Colonies. 'The Conservatives, with minor differences in emphasis', the *Times* says, 'can subscribe to every word of it'. That, in itself, should be enough to condemn it out of hand as a Socialist pronouncement . . .

"Why should the Welsh people and the Welsh workers soil their hands in this bloody business, even if the English people support and enjoy it? I am quite certain that the Welsh workers generally, moulded as they are in a nobler tradition, will not endorse this tory pronouncement. We must have something better than this."

★ ★ ★

"Our readers will remember that we spot-lighted the cause of Cyprus long before it became news . . . " reads the editorial preface to this article under the title 'CYPRUS IN CHAINS' by Stefos Paladios, a Greek journalist then living in Wales. And here at the end of this century, in all its topicality it emerges for presentation again:

"Never before has Britain faced such a devastating problem as the question of Cyprus seeking Enosis, or Union with Greece.

"Cyprus is not a newly discovered territory. It is a part of the Hellenistic civilisation of more than 3,000 years ago, at a time when England was not even a geographical expression.

"The island since has had many masters, and since 1914 has been a Crown colony.

"Anyone taking into account all these invasions would wonder about the nationality of the inhabitants. Yet in spite of all these strong influences, Cypriots remained true to their forefathers, conserving intact all the traditions of a truly Grecian character. Their language remains Greek through thousands of years, so do their customs, mentality, religion and aspirations.

"During the Turkish occupation which lasted some 200 years, many attempts were made to introduce into the island thousands of Turkish immigrants. The experiment failed and many of them had to return to Turkey, whilst most of those left had to learn Greek to survive.

"The English occupation at the day of reckoning after the first and second Great Wars when all the Greek populated territories were liberated and re-united with Greece, prevented the liberation also of Cyprus which remained under English domination.

"Now which is the position, how does the problem of ENOSIS stand? Only a few days ago the autocratic government of Cyprus revived the vicious anti-seditious law by which no-one, under the penalty of imprisonment and fine, could simply utter the word Enosis, and must not even discuss the subject.

"Simultaneously, the Minister for the Colonies declared in the Commons that Cyprus was one of the colonies which could never gain its independence, and that no talks could be held on the future of

Cyprus with the Greek Government.

"Cyprus today is governed by the grace and decrees of its Governor and his advisers, like the most backward colony. The people of Cyprus have no voice and are never consulted.

"The great majority of the Cypriots have lost faith in any kind of constitution and demand Enosis and only Enosis.

"Finally, on August 20th the Greek government by a note, requested the Secretary of UNO to discuss Cyprus. Britain, adopting a completely negative attitude, will claim that the subject is of a domestic character and therefore UNO is not competent to discuss it.

"Here are some points in favour of Enosis:

1. Four-fifths of the Cypriots are Greek in every sense.
2. The Turkish government never objected to Enosis.
3. Cyprus is the most advanced British colony, with 78% literacy; 85% of its officials, lawyers, physicians and other professions are Cypriots.
4. Its liberation would not produce any gap or chaos, as the island would be integrated into the political and economic system of the mother country.
5. The Greek Government repeatedly declared that it is willing to grant any bases that Britain requires, not only in Cyprus, but any part of Greece.

★ ★ ★

By the end of 1954 *Y Gweriniaethwr* itself was the soul and substance of the Welsh Republican Movement. It was a production of which all Republicans had reason to be greatly proud. Its circulation was enthusiastically promoted via its pages, and its distribution and despatch to all subscribers carefully attended to from, by now, the City Road base in Caerdydd. Editorship was now the sole preserve of the *Dewin* of Dowlais, and so it remained to the end of the paper's life.

The last name in the register of distribution is numbered 619, and is that of one, Alun Hughes, Dudlow Lane, Liverpool 18. Is it too much perhaps, to suggest that in that fact Alun, of Republican convictions it is hoped, may have achieved some little measure of immortality'? . . . To look back over those long lists, and in particular the names of the many who responded so generously to the appeals for funds to meet fines inflicted, brings a mood of hiraeth for a generation of patriots who, in great part, must no longer be with us.

Because *The Welsh Republican* was not now sold on the streets and in the pubs to the same extent as before in the heyday of political activity, it became necessary by the end of 1954 to reduce the number printed to 1,000 copies of each issue. Publication remained at that figure up to the time of the last print of 750 for April-May 1957. Apart from the first two issues of the paper in 1950, its printing had been in the hands of the firm of Brook & Williams, Y Barri. And to them, under their very helpful and friendly proprietor, Mr Ken Jones, all those of the Republican faith in Cymru must be for ever indebted.

However, after the heyday of their activity, for various reasons any effective staging by the Republicans of their ardent convictions on the familiar streets and squares of the Valley towns had to come to an end. Most members of the Movement, a few in relief perhaps, turned their eyes towards quieter political pastures; but always in the hope of finding in those directions some way to fulfilment of their nationalist ideals. Some joined the Labour party and fought local government elections in its name. A notable instance, of course, was Gwilym Prys Davies, who fought the parliamentary seat of Caerfyrddin for the Labour party in 1966. Others of the Republicans found themselves 'marking time', as it were, not able as yet to move towards any other party.

But it was Plaid Cymru that eventually claimed most of them and came to enjoy their faithful allegiance. Harri Webb fought a parliamentary seat in Gwent for Plaid Cymru. Others frequently stood as candidates for the Blaid in local government election and came to, and still do, hold office in constituency and branch organizations and so on.

★ ★ ★

And now at last to face up to the question that must be asked — what, if anything, of enduring worth to the cause of Cymru has been left for us in the sometimes stormy wake of those young Republicans about whom this story has been recorded?

On the way towards the answer, perhaps it can be of help to quote, first the opinion of one, Alan Butt Philip, an observer of presumably some degree of impartiality: "In one important respect, despite its evident failure, the Welsh Republican Movement could claim long-term success. Plaid Cymru in the 60s was surely changing into the sort of party the Republicans had wanted it to be in 1948; that is, a party that was more secular, and more interested in the Welsh economy than in the Welsh culture in isolation. Whereas in 1948 Plaid Cymru was unable to keep within its ranks men and women who wanted to see these changes, such people were in 1968 the moving spirits in the Nationalist movement."

And then — the opinion of someone who by no means could be judged impartial. Harri Webb himself, in review has said: "It is no coincidence that

Plaid Cymru's advance in the Valleys in the 60s was in precisely those areas laboriously evangelized by the Republicans in the 50s. Perhaps Nationalist Wales at the time was too small to offer the necessary room for manoeuvre between possible alternative leadership cadres. Certainly, any attempt at criticism was bitterly resented as base disloyalty . . . Another service Republicans could be said to have performed for the Nationalist cause was to secede, and sustain serious activity for the best part of a decade."

Here, at least, are two opinions from presumably different standpoints which seem in important respects to coincide.

For a balanced reasoned assessment of the Movement's significance in Welsh politics of its time one could do no better than to look first at the reactions and attitudes of political parties and their personalities who came under its lash.

The activity and rhetoric of the Movement had undoubtedly further consolidated Tory party thinking in its already implacable opposition towards any idea of self-determination for the Welsh nation. A fact which, because of the antipathy of the great majority of the Welsh people to Toryism, could only redound to the eventual advantage of the nationalist cause in Wales.

On the other hand, the Labour party, attacked by the Movement in the surprise and disgust of seeing it more than ready to take over in effect many of the trappings of English empire from Tory shoulders, could never be said to be a party united in that rôle. In particular, many prominent members of the Labour party in Wales were strong and determined dissidents from the official labour party policy on the matter of political devolution for Wales.

As witness to this, was the fervent and sincere support given by much respected Welsh Labour leaders to the Campaign in the early 1950s under the presidency of Megan Lloyd George for a Parliament for Wales. The names of Dic Beamish, Cwm Tawe, and the eloquent Gwyn Phillips, Ystradmynach, important figures in the mining community of the Valleys, stand out in particular in this context. And who is to say that it was not the Welsh Republican Movement in the uncompromising boldness of its political stance that helped to add fire to the words and endeavours of these and other radical Labour party members in the cause of Wales, and perhaps even set the initial spark to the waiting tinder of patriotism in them.

At the 1954 Welsh Miners' Conference in Porthcawl, through the instrumentality of those such as Dic Beamish, Gwyn Phillips, and Huw T. Edwards from the North, the issue of a Parliament for Wales was debated for the first time by the miners in Conference. Most of the delegates voted against the idea. But the number in favour was far from negligible and, as was suggested in *The Welsh Republican* at the time, many of the still larger proportion who abstained were most probably prompted by the wish not to have to vote against Dai Grenfell and Jim Griffiths, deputed by Labour HQ to speak against the proposition in Porth-cawl.

At this time, some six Labour MPs from Wales had given formal, sometimes active, support to the Campaign, to which Cliff Bere of the Republican Movement had been appointed South-East Wales organizer in July 1954.

In 1964 the new Labour government created the office of Secretary of State for Wales, with James Griffiths occupying its title rôle. Who, again, is to say that the coming into being of that office was not in some measure at least due to the hardly forgotten experiences suffered by its first holder at the hands of the Young Republicans a decade or so earlier?

Already, before the end of 1953 the editorial of *The Welsh Republican* was confidently able to say: "Under the stimulus of competition both Plaid Cymru and the Welsh Labour movement have improved out of all recognition . . . " — with this pronouncement of course having particular reference to Plaid Cymru as a party having objectives directly akin to those of the WRM. There is no doubt that the tempo of activities in Plaid Cymru had been stimulated by the bolder, more challenging attitude of the Republicans. *The Welsh Republican* was read and admired by many in Plaid Cymru, who realized that a new standard of militancy in the national cause had been demonstrated, and which they themselves had to try to follow in their own way so that new, broader horizons had to be explored and ventured upon. That was the legacy which those nationalists who could appreciate it inherited from the Young Republicans, and to which some of the greater political success of Plaid Cymru in later years could in part be attributed.

In the more actionist field of nationalist politics in Wales the Republican precedent seemed to have set in motion over the following decades a train of events which has helped to bring the cause of self-government for Wales more and more into prominence in the political scene in Britain. If the Welsh Republican Movement itself had ceased to play an active part in that process, it had yet served a valuable purpose and made its contribution to the progress of the freedom movement in modern Wales.

Perhaps, however, it is against a context of longer term extending back for generations into the often heroic past, and all-importantly ahead into the expectant future that the efforts of those young Republicans can best be judged. If it was not they who started the tradition of aspiration to shake off, together with their nation's state of subjection, the alien, outrageous symbol of it, then, it was they who renewed that tradition.

And in due course, in 1973, *Y Gweriniaethwr — The Welsh Republican* made its appearance again. "After over 15 years of silence *Y Gweriniaethwr* speaks out again in the name of Welsh radicalism," the editorial began, " . . . This newspaper is the voice of The Welsh Republican Movement; the Republican Movement is committed to the capture by the people of Wales of full political and economic sovereignty . . . We stand for the restoration of the Welsh language to its rightful position as the first language of Wales, because we regard the language as the basis of Welsh Nationhood — if the language is not restored, then the nation will not be restored. We stand for the placing of the control of the economy of Wales into the hands of the people of Wales, because the people of Wales produce the wealth of Wales, and the control of that wealth must be theirs . . . "

This first issue of the new publication, dated August-September 1973, had linked itself as Vol. 8 No. 1 in rightful succession to the original series. It made effective use of old copy from that series, and took new material from its former contributors to say, for example:

> "In England itself a growing number of radical-minded politicians await their chance to vent their distaste for the royalist system. Already in their minds they are adjusting to a republican future. And in England, as in Cymru, a new sort of generation is graduating towards political responsibility. Change is coming that will bring a new fashion in government in England sooner than ever imagined a generation ago. From the standpoint of Republicans in Cymru, the vital factor of the situation is the chance and the responsibility it gives us to set the pace of events by showing that English royalism is even less relevant to the future of Cymru. For us, Republicanism will be more than just a constitutional change of fashion slogan, it will be the symbol of the revolution from which there can be no escaping if we intend to win our freedom."

But for the most part, the new production was in the hands of a newer generation. It was very ably and almost immaculately produced. The printers of its first issue were, again, that estimable firm of Brook & Williams, Y Barri. Subsequent issues were no less immaculately, and even more expansively, printed as well as published by the Welsh Republican Movement itself. This new series persisted defiantly for some half-a-dozen issues, until the ineluctable laws of economic survival brought it to an end.

Later in the 70s a radical paper, *Y Faner Goch (Red Flag)*, with 'For a Welsh Socialist Republic' sharing its title at the masthead, came into print. This substantial publication, fluctuating between Welsh and English in the presentation of its message, has continued in successful production up into the 90s.

At the end of the 70s also, appeared *The Welsh Republic* as organ of the Welsh Socialist Republican Movement. The paper and the Movement maintained publication and activity in the field of Republican Socialist propaganda for several years.

In the mid-80s a reputable and independent commentator on the political scene in Cymru was able to speak of "the network of Welsh Socialist

Republican Clubs currently being set up . . . The first has already been formed in Gwent, one is being established in Cardiff in January, and others are being formed in the Rhymney Valley, in Swansea, Merthyr, Newtown, Aberystwyth and Flint. The term 'Club' has been deliberately adopted to distance the movement from conventional political activity such as fighting elections. So far, about 200 people (probably more) are actively involved in organising such Clubs across Wales. They are mainly young people who are either members of Plaid Cymru or who have had links with the party in the past, but there are others too, connected with the Labour Party and the Communists."

★ ★ ★

The bold, hardly dared to be uttered ambition that must have burned in the hearts of our rebellious and so often heroic and martyred kin in the last century has more than survived into the later years of this. In that process the young Republicans of our mid-century are not to be begrudged their part.

And now the expectant future awaits.

Chapter 22

A BRIEF SELECTION FROM THE PAGES OF THE LATER ISSUES OF THE WELSH REPUBLICAN — Y GWERINIAETHWR

December, 1954 — January, 1955

> Glorious Figures from our Past . . . or what they don't allow to be taught in Welsh Schools.

LEWSYN YR HELIWR (*LEWIS THE HUNTSMAN*)

Welsh History is full of vivid pictures — and none more dramatic than the contrast between the two young leaders of the Merthyr Rising of 1831 — between Dic Penderyn and Lewis Lewis, known as Lewis the Huntsman. The one seems to move in an aura of innocence that time has transformed into the halo of martyrdom. The other a creature of mystery and night, walks in violence, and disappears into the dark.

We first meet him when the Rising is in full swing. Dic Penderyn's irregulars, armed with furnace-bars and pitch-forks have put to flight the Swansea Yeomanry, and taken their weapons; they have ambushed the troops from Brecon and scared off those from Cardiff. A flag dipped in blood has been paraded through the narrow, twisting streets of Merthyr. Within the gleaming new stonework of Cyfarthfa Castle huddle the ironmasters; the brassy, blustering men from England are squealing like rats. That night Lewis the Huntsman hunts with a deep-tongued pack indeed. The furnaces are drawn in Cyfarthfa and Penydarren, the glare goes out on Dowlais Hill. And to the unaccustomed stars shoots up a new fire, the flames of Vengeance as the houses of the oppressors are burnt by the people and the Court of Injustice laid low.

But next day the soldiers get through — simple Scotch mercenaries from the Outer Isles, victims themselves of hunger and oppression. They huddle like sheep in the crowded streets. The masters are bold now. They read the Riot Act from an upstairs window. Lewis the Huntsman is there to lead the hunt again. The soldiers are hemmed in and overwhelmed as he urges resistance and strikes the first blow. A soldier is wounded. Dic Penderyn will hang for this on the evidence of a lying barber, and Lewis will stand his trial and deportation. For the play is almost played, and soon it is the turn of the smooth, hard men with the big battalions at their backs. The Lancers will ride in while the Welsh dead lie in the streets, and the Taff runs mourning by the silent slums . . .

We do not know what happened to Lewis the Huntsman after his banishment. We do not need to know. His pack hunts yet!

YOU ARE NEEDED FOR IT!

★ ★ ★

February — March, 1955

    Glorious Figures from our Past . . . or what they don't allow to be taught in Welsh Schools.

SHONI 'SGUBORFAWR

Maybe John Jones the ex-prizefighter of Merthyr was not one of the great figures of the Welsh 19th century. But he was one of the most colourful, swashbuckling characters that ever took aim at an English soldier. Shoni 'Sguborfawr — that was how he was known throughout West Wales, this huge fist-battered man whose vast bulk people likened to a barn.

It was Rebecca who weaned Shoni from his prizefighting, Rebecca who captured his imagination, the same Rebecca who freed the roads of Wales from tolls, who attacked the workhouses in protest against the Poor Law, Rebecca of the nights, Rebecca of the lightning thrust, Rebecca of bold plan and sure execution, Rebecca to whom the Welsh people turned for justice. And Shoni fought for Rebecca for 5sh. a day. In the cause of the people Shoni was daring, taut for action, ruthless. It was Shoni who schemed to mine the road over which the proud peacocking English Dragoons were to pass. And when a meeting of anti-Rebecca elements was held on Mynydd Sylen, hard above Llan-non, Shoni was there, large as life, and most conspicuously agreeing that the power of Rebecca must indeed be curbed. But when night fell over the grey hills, it was Shoni who loaded his gun, grimly, silently, and went hunting those who had dared to condemn the idol of the Welsh, the dispenser of justice. And it was Shoni too, who, in the small hours of one morning, led an attack on Pontyberem ironworks, and warned the overbearing English manager to be out of Wales within the week. Shoni's deeds had small need to grow in the telling . . .

Then, when Shoni was captured — where else but in a small, low-ceilinged, sawdust-floored Welsh inn, a pint of beer before him, a loaded gun beside him? A whole company of English soldiers guarded Carmarthen jail when Shoni was there, and London police armed with cutlasses ringed the Town Hall when he was tried. Shoni looked very attentive when the learned judge gave his address, and when he was sentenced to transportation for life, this hard-living, life-loving, hard-fighting Welshman left the dock, laughing. In February 1844 we catch our last glimpse of Shoni 'Sguborfawr, waiting his ship in Millbank Penitentiary, far from the tangled hills and the warm peasant laughter of West Wales. The battle was over for Shoni. But the battle of Wales, that eternal inheritance of the Welsh generations, goes on . . . YOU ARE NEEDED FOR IT!

* * *

April — May, 1955
Glorious Figures from our Past . . . or what they don't allow to be taught in Welsh Schools.

DAI'R CANTWR

When David Davies (Dai'r Cantwr) was born in Llancarfan, where Welsh Scholars had once chronicled the deeds of our princes, the whitewashed cottages of the Garden of Wales were still trellised with vines, and old Iolo Morgannwg nearby was gathering great sheaves of song from the lore of the past and the lips of living people. But already to the north, the pillar of cloud by day and fire by night hung over the valleys where that people were treading a path through the wilderness of the Age of Iron.

Soon Dai was in Tredegar and Ebbw Vale. The songs he had sung behind the ox-plough gave way to a deeper music, and when the currents of the iron trade took him down west to Pontyberem he was on the threshold of a new destiny. For Rebecca was riding through the land, and the singer from the Vale became one of her stoutest sons. With Shoni 'Sguborfawr he was one of the full-time soldiers of the Goddess of the Night.

He had won his name by teaching singing in the chapels. Now he taught Wales a song she was never to forget. He was associated with Shoni 'Sguborfawr in all his exploits and was finally captured and tried at the same time.

Now came the reckoning. Eleven years of hard labour and exile, and the rest of his life a broken sequence of obscure, casual jobs. Somewhere in the paupers' corner of the churchyard at Ross is the nettle-grown grave of a poor old fellow who died in the barn of the hotel where charity had given him a bed of straw. Such is the price Wales demands of those who serve her. Such has been the cold end of so many of her soldiers.

Dai Cantwr's bones lie beyond the Dyke, but his memory lives in the green

heart of our land, and Wales has never lacked for those who do not count the cost of serving her. For the struggle of Rebecca and her Children is the struggle of all the Children of Wales . . .
>   YOU ARE NEEDED FOR IT!

★ ★ ★

August — September, 1955

COLLED I GYMRU
Mrs Elizabeth Rhys Evans, Y Bala
Hunodd Gorffennaf 10fed 1955

Bu farw Mrs Elis Evans, Y Bala, yr haf hwn ar ôl dioddefaint hir, ac y mae ei theulu a Chymru gyfan wedi colli cymeriad cryf a hawddgar. Hi oedd hoff ŵyres Michael D. Jones, a dolen fyw â'r gwladgarwr mawr hwnnw. Etifeddodd hi ei ysbryd ef, a gweithiodd yn rymus dros ei chenedl. Addas, felly, oedd iddi hi a'i phriod fod ymhlith aelodau cyntaf Mudiad Gweriniaethol Cymru, ac yn gymwynaswyr cyson iddo. Claddwyd llwch Mrs Evans ym medd ei thaid, Michael D. Jones, ond erys ei choffadwriaeth yn galondid i bawb a'i hadwaenai.

★ ★ ★

WARNING TO WELSH INDUSTRY
Automation and the Future

A few years ago not many of us were familiar with such words as cybernetics, transistors, servo-mechs and automation. But such is the speed with which technology is transforming our lives that these ideas have literally stepped out overnight from the pages of science-fiction and their impact on the wage-packet of the Welsh worker cannot long be delayed.

Automation is the current magician — and bogey. For this technique, by which whole assembly lines are regulated and worked by one or two electronic robots, has many implications, the plainest of which is: *big money on repetitive jobs in the light and secondary industries is at an end in the foreseeable future.*

Other considerations are:

A reduced labour force;

Reorganisation and re-deployment of unskilled labour, with the likelihood of unemployment for those least qualified to compete in the labour market.

Reduction in labour costs per finished article, by which it will be impossible for the non-automation concern to compete commercially. (What effect here on

Remploy and Grenfell factories?)

Necessity for re-deployment of Capital and a possible wholesale reorganisation of industry — the most serious threat of all to the prosperity of industrial Wales.

Even the most rabidly anti-Welsh MPs and journalists have never attempted to ignore the fact that the 'new' industries in Wales are mostly offshoots of English firms. (They would if they could, of course.) The instability of, and lack of deep confidence in, the new industries is a marked feature of the most ordinary conversation anywhere in Wales these days, and now as if to confirm these doubts, come the first tidings of a new phase of the Industrial Revolution, which may have the gravest short-term consequences for a large section of the working population, and even worse long-term effects on the economic potential of Wales.

An independent country with our resources (and this includes our people, who, working in many cases with similar tools to the Americans, show much better results) need fear no advance in technology. But as things are, we are at the mercy of events.

We want to hear of Welsh Trade Unionists meeting to discuss Automation in relation to the light industries on the Trading Estates and elsewhere.

We want to hear of the Council for Wales empanelling a special committee to enquire into the financial and social consequences which can be so easily foreseen.

We want to hear of the National and Local Education Authorities of Wales pressing for enhanced facilities for technical education to meet the demand for men versed in the new skills.

Above all, we want to hear of a general demand, enforced with all the might of organized Labour, that Wales shall control its own economic resources and its own industrial policy, and be free not only from present exploitation, but from future forebodings.

★ ★ ★

Glorious Figures from our Past . . .

IEUAN GWYNEDD

Often in Welsh history have men of peaceful ways struck as hard a blow for their country as any soldier in the field. From Giraldus to Iolo, the bards and scholars, the lawyers and clergy, provided they never forgot the people from whom they were sprung, have deserved well of Wales — none more so than Ieuan Gwynedd. To some today he may seem a dated figure: a minister very much concerned with the outmoded preoccupations of the Nonconformist conscience.

But he loved Wales with such passion that he consumed his frail physique in her service and occupies a very special place in the affections of all patriots. He seems, at first sight to have had a shabby deal from life, the child of poverty, the nurseling of narrow Puritanism, the victim of the current second-rate standards in prose and verse, the constant prey of ill-health and the killing disease our fathers called 'consumption'. From Merioneth out to Tredegar, London and Cardiff, from ill-paid job to job in press and pulpit, from obscure lodgings to a neglected grave; such was one aspect of his earthly pilgrimage.

But he never ceased to glorify Wales and proclaim her redemption. To his congregation at Tredegar he bade farewell by telling them to place their country under the rule of Christ, not of Victoria. His language may not be quite ours, but his sentiments are unmistakeable.

He criticized the Imperialism of England bitterly, but co-operated to found a famous English publishing house. And above all he led the national agitation against the infamous 'Blue Books' which sought to extirpate the Welsh language in the name of 'Education'. His verse burst out of the inflated idiom of the period into brilliant satirical ballads pillorying the bishops and alien commissioners. He conducted a one-man campaign throughout Wales, and did as much as one man could do to arouse a nation.

Ieuan Gwynedd's epitaph has not been written by the booby 'scholars' to whom he was a 'sickly, febrile and vehement agitator'. But there is one obvious act of homage which the nation can pay him. He was clearly the most important man who lodged in a modest Cardiff back-street, since become part of a massive new boulevard, one of the features of the city. This thoroughfare is at present disgraced with the name of 'Churchill Way'. We feel sure that in due course this insult to Wales will be removed and the new road re-named 'Ffordd Ieuan Gwynedd' as it should have been from the first — one more act of belated justice to be performed in the march of our country to independence. YOU ARE NEEDED FOR IT!

* * *

October — November, 1955

LLUOEDD ARFOG I GYMRU

Dyfodol y genedl Gymreig a thwf y mudiad cenedlaethol yw'r ddwy ystyriaeth bwysicaf wrth drafod gorfodaeth filwrol. Daeth Chris Rees o'r carchar ddiwedd Awst ar ôl gwneud cyfraniad cryf i'r traddodiad o wrthsafiad Cymreig. Yr egwyddor genedlaethol bur yw nad oes hawl gan fwyafrif o Saeson i orfodi gwasanaeth milwrol ar Gymry ifainc mewn lluoedd arfog sydd, i bob pwrpas, yn sefydliadau hollol Seisnig. Ar y llaw arall, er bod cryn anfodlonrwydd ar gonsgripsiwn fel y mae, yn Lloegr yn ogystal ag yng Nghymru ar hyn o bryd, nid yw'n debyg o ddod i ben eto. Pery anghenion strategol Lloegr yn gyfryw ag i hawlio lluoedd arfog annaturiol o gryf.

Y mae terfynau clir i'r hyn y gellir ei gyrraedd drwy wrthwynebiad cydwybodol unigolion. Peth peryglus weithiau yw gofyn triniaeth arbennig, yn arbennig wrth geisio hybu mudiad cenedlaethol. Yn wir, y mae cryn dipyn i'w ddweud dros gyfnod o wasanaeth milwrol neu gymdeithasol, yng Nghymru yn anad unman, fel y gwelodd gwŷr doeth fel D.J. Williams a Saunders Lewis o'r cychwyn. Angen Cymru yw elwa ar y drefn bresennol. Gallai gorfodaeth filwrol wneud llawer o waith ymarferol i uno'r genhedlaeth ifanc mewn gwladgarwch Cymreig iachus. Dylid felly geisio Cymreigio'r lluoedd arfog yn eu perthynas â gwaith amddiffyn Cymreig y wladwriaeth bresennol.

Da iawn y gwna'r Cyngor Ymgynghorol Cymreig wrth anfon Syr Ifan ab Owen a Mr John Clement i ymweled ag unedau o'r fyddin yng Nghymru, i sicrhau bod Cymry Cymraeg yn cael chwarae teg. Wrth gwrs, nid yw hyn ond cyffwrdd â'r ymylon. Y gwir angen yw Lluoedd Arfog Cymreig cyflawn, â'u pencadlysoedd a'u meysydd ymarfer a'u canolfannau tir, môr ac awyr yng Nghymru. Byddai'n ddiddorol gwybod a alwodd Cyngor Cymru ar rai o'r Cadfridogion ac o'r swyddogion eraill o fri yn y Llu Awyr a'r Llynges Brydeinig, sy'n Gymry, i drafod y dulliau gorau o sefydlu Lluoedd Cymreig oddi mewn i'r gyfundrefn bresennol. Eisoes, cyhoeddodd y Cyngor adroddiadau o fudd mawr. Byddai adroddiad cynhwysfawr ar orfodaeth filwrol a'r moddion i'w chymhwyso at ofynion Lluoedd Arfog Cymreig parhaol yn gyfraniad pwysicach fyth at ddiogelu dyfodol Cymru.
H.D.

★ ★ ★

Glorious Figures from our Past . . .

ZEPHANIAH WILLIAMS

The great Welsh Rising of 1839 produced many gifted men, sprung from the people to lead the people. There was John Frost, the most famous of them, the shoemaker's son who had become Mayor of Newport, William Jones, the orator, who led the men of Pontypool, the colourful Dr William Price, in charge of the Merthyr and Dowlais contingents, there was George Shell who fell to the bullets of the English soldiery (you will not find *his* name in the Cymrodorion sponsored Dictionary of National Biography, widely known as the 'Parchgraffiadur'), and there was *Zephaniah Williams*. Not a well-known public figure like John Frost, not a glamour-boy like the incredible Doctor, not a rash youth like Shell, not an orator like Jones, but a man perhaps with more ability than any of them — perhaps indeed the real architect of the Rising which more than most struck fear into the hearts of the alien capitalists and their rich Welsh hangers-on. Williams, the Blaina pub-keeper, the free-thinker, the pillar of the Workingmen's Association, was a mature 44 when he led the men of Blaina, Nant-y-glo and Ebbw Vale down to Nine-Mile Point on that tragic and stormy night of 1839, old enough to remember the fate of Dic Penderyn eight years previous, but strong enough to organise and march nevertheless. The Rising failed. Williams was captured on board ship in the New Docks at Cardiff, proof of the rebels well-laid plans to cover all emergencies; and with Frost and Jones he was sentenced to the barbarous and gruesome penalties for High Treason. But even the corrupt government of England knew better than to enforce this hideous fate. The three leaders were sent across the sea to the then unimaginably distant penal colony of Tasmania. And it is gratifying to record that at least one of the great leaders of the Welsh Fighting Century was able to turn the tables on his enemies. For Williams, who had been connected with the mines all his life, soon saw that there was coal to be had in Tasmania. He became a rich man through his discoveries, and a benefactor to the land to which he was forbidden to return. His is the doughty, deep-thinking, never-say-die spirit that is needed for the next stage in the liberation of Wales.

YOU ARE NEEDED FOR IT!

* * *

December, 1955 — January, 1956

THE FRONTIER OF WALES

Plaid Cymru is determined to contest all the Parliamentary seats "in Wales", — in number 36. An excellent resolve.

These 36 constituencies are not, however, coterminous with the national territory of Wales. There are areas at present the far side of the so-called "Welsh-border", and adjacent to that 'border', which are as much a part of our territory as is Gower or Lleyn. Areas around Oswestry and South of Hereford for instance.

The county boundaries and the present so-called "Welsh border" were set up by commissioners of the English King during the time when Wales was being subjected and parcelled out. It would be ludicrous to allow that the pickings and overlordings of apostates and foreigners should have settled the geographical extent of our country.

Once enlightened historical investigation has shown where the national frontier shall properly lie, it will behove Plaid Cymru to extend its electoral fight to all areas within that frontier.

And if the enemies of Wales, within and without, raise a protracted quibbling about the validity of this proper frontier, then let it be made clear to them that Wales will accept as an alternative, not the frontier of their hostile fabrication, but rather the only frontier ever agreed upon by a Welsh national leader free from conditions of duress and fraud, namely the agreement of 1405 between Owain Glyndŵr and the English, placing the frontier of Wales on the line of the Dee and the Severn.

J.L.

* * *

MICE OR MEN?

In some of the less momentous human affairs the quality of naivete can have a charm all of its own. When it is to be found however in the political affairs of a nation, and in particular of a nation fighting for its life, the charm is not so apparent — except perhaps to the would-be destroyers of the nation in question. It took the outbreak of war and the impact of disaster to open the eyes of England to the political naivete of Mr Neville Chamberlain. Similarly with Wales, it seems that she will have to be in the very last ditch of desperation before she gets the leadership she needs.

The recent much publicized reaffirmation by the President of Plaid Cymru (in a speech in Anglesey) of the pacifist policy of his party is, to say the least, disheartening. Not so much because of the President's personal and already well-known pacifist views, but because of the lack of political realism which such a public utterance displays. Indeed, it provides (by comparison) an object-lesson in the essential quality of realism that must distinguish a man before he can become not merely the leader of his party, but of his nation.

"I have only to lift my finger to plunge Ireland into blood," said Parnell, the leader of Ireland, to the English government. No one was more sickened by violence and bloodshed than Parnell, and no one was less likely to have carried out that threat. Before everything, however, he was determined to make the fullest advantage of each card that was in his hand to play. That there were men in Ireland (as there are in every nation) who were ready to fight for the nation's life was an ace in that hand. But although Parnell did not play the card, he did not throw it away with any pious public utterances. He kept it in his hand, and because it was there, kept the wholesome respect of Ireland's enemies.

Before the last war, Czechoslovakia, proud and vigorous in her new won independence, was a source of inspiration to us in Wales. The histories of our

two countries had run in a striking parallel through the centuries. In temperament and quality and history the Welsh and the Czechs seem to be more akin to one another than any other people on earth. Listen to the words of Hitler during the Nazi occupation of Czechoslovakia:
"They're skilled at not awakening the distrust of their occupiers and are wonderful at playing the role of subject. It's true they've had five centuries of it!"

They might be the words of Churchill — or almost any London prime minister — about the Welsh.

And pursuing the parallel, with a further quotation from Hitler:

> "We must therefore give a categorical no in reply to the Czech aspiration for the creation of a national army, even for an army in embryo. Servile for as long as he is unarmed, the Czech becomes dangerously arrogant when he is allowed to don uniform . . . One realizes the extent to which the bearing of arms contributes to a nation's pride and bearing when one compares the Czechs of 1938 with those incarnations of servility whom one finds in the country today."

In the name of Wales let us not ignore the lesson!
C.B.

* * *

December, 1955 — January, 1956
Glorious Figures from our Past . . .
DR WILLIAM PRICE

Few will deny Dr William Price his place in the crowded and colourful gallery of great Welsh eccentrics. But many will be rather surprised to find him numbered among the heroes and martyrs. Wasn't he the rambustious old rodney who went about in a flamboyant costume of his own design which would have left a Teddy-boy gasping? Didn't he invent a new religion which incorporated nudism, vegetarianism, druidry and cremation? Wasn't he always engaged in fantastic lawsuits which were the delight of the ordinary man and the despair of the legal profession? Yes he did all of these things. He exhumed his father's body and sent the skull to the lawyers to disprove the validity of his will. He begat a child at an age when most people have retired from such activities. He carried out an exhibitionistic funeral ceremony on Pontypridd Common (thereby, incidentally, establishing and legality of cremation). In fact he was well worth the place of honour which his widely distributed likeness enjoys in the bar parlours of Mid-Glamorgan.

But he has claims to a higher honour. With his great gifts he could have been a fashionable physician, basking in the favours of the rich. Yet he cast his lot with the misery of the valleys, lavishing his skill on the broken bodies of the victims of alien capitalism, who he knew could never afford to pay him. And when the Great Rising of 1839 shook the land, Price was there. He it was who spoke out most forcefully and clearly to express the driving revolutionary spirit behind the Chartist Movement. And he it was whom the men of Dowlais and Merthyr Tydfil elected to lead them into battle. Poseur and exhibitionist he was, but it could have been no mere mountebank whom those dour and determined men chose to bestride the saddle of the Huntsman and to wield the sword of Dic Penderyn. These were men who had paid the price of that immortal failure eight years previously. They knew what they were up against, and Price, their friend and healer, knew it too.

The history of that November night is still as dark as the storm that overwhelmed it and destroyed the Army of the Valleys before it could reach Newport. The movements of the heavily armed Merthyr contingent remain a mystery. But the English Government were under no illusions about the Doctor. With a price on his head (an honour that few Welshmen have achieved) he got away to Swansea and boarded a boat for Liverpool. Here he caught a train to London and took ship for France, calmly walking through the heart of a metropolis which his activities had reduced to panic. He lived for a long time after that, returning to Wales when the hue and cry had died down, getting his name in the papers for his weird carryings-on, a gift to the ballad-makers at fair and market, execrated by the respectable but loved by the people, for he breathed their own spirit of challenge and revolt, and had been identified with one of the great moments in their struggle.

That struggle goes on.

YOU ARE NEEDED FOR IT!

February — March, 1956

From — GLEANINGS BY THE WAY

But Who Went First?
"The days of the Welsh language are at an end."
The late Dr Thomas Jones, C.H.

Largo Al Factotum
Music is normally banned in the House, but the gathering was allowed to wind up with 'Hen Wlad fy Nhadau', led by Mr James Griffiths, who, in his immaculate full evening dress, reminded one very forcibly of a famous operatic tenor.
The Western Mail

From the Correspondence Column:

THE FRONTIERS OF WALES

Your article on the Frontier was right. I was born only a few miles from Oswestry, and some three miles from Sycharth, the home of Glyndŵr. Oswestry has been called 'England' since 1536, but it is more Welsh than many a town within the present borders of Wales. Here we really see 'Cambria Irredenta'. Think of the place-names now supposed to be in Shropshire: Llynclys, Nantmawr, Treflach, Trefonnen, Creiglwyn, Selattyn (where the great poet Goronwy Owen was once a curate), Bronygarth, Coedygo, Llanforda, Llanblodwch, Porthywaun . . . All these districts are very different from the rest of Shropshire. To the east of Oswestry there is a witches' kitchen of anti-Welsh feeling and narrow, servile prejudice. If I should forget thee, Oswestry . . .

E. Jones, Denbigh.

April — May, 1956

Glorious Figures from Our Past . . .

LEWIS HUMPHREYS - BUGLER OF LIBERTY

'THE HORN OF LIBERTY sounded for the attendance of the populace on the Long Bridge across the Severn by Llanidloes, where they were addressed by speakers from the parapets, after which they hurried to the rescue of their comrades, apprehended for training, or acquiring the art of self defence . . . '

Thus wrote Hugh Williams, Chartist and Rebeccaite. For these were stirring days in Powys. On the one hand, Lord Powys feasting in the Red Castle of the March, on the other, Catherine Owen, eaten by rats as she starved to death. (Verdict: died by the visitation of God). On the one hand, God's plenty in "Powys Paradwys Cymru", on the other — enclosures, game-laws, and the workhouse Bastilles. There was the promise of prosperity as new industrial techniques were applied to the woollen mills, but then came the **Credit Squeeze** of the London Bankers, and unemployment. (How history repeats itself!) Then to Newtown, birthplace of Robert Owen, to Llanidloes, and to Welshpool in the shadow of the Red Castle, came the People's Charter, brought by local men, Charles Jones and Richard Jarman. Then came drilling in the hills and gatherings in the narrow streets, and a story not yet fully told of comedy and mystery, heroism and tragedy: the mystery of the weapons that were collected for a shooting match that never came off, the comedy of the English policemen, smuggled in as invalids, and who were found hiding in corners when things got rough, the unbelievable Mayor, who was dragged out from under a bed by the men he had mocked, the clergyman-magistrate inciting the troops to massacre the workers — and the troops refusing!

The Horn of Liberty was a tin bugle belonging to a man called Baxter, but the Bugler of Liberty was LEWIS HUMPHREYS. At its sound the workers rallied, released their arrested comrades and took over the town, where they ruled for a week with perfect discipline and order (having first poured all the booze into the gutter), thus shaming their "betters", the dissolute and incompetent "gentry". Finally over-awed by a great display of force, the Independent Commune of Llanidloes collapsed, but not before rebels by the score were over the hills to Merthyr Tydfil, "the haven of all discontented spirits", to march again with John Frost in the winter of that year. Lewis Humphreys was transported to Van Diemen's Land, but not before his battered tin bugle had aroused from the hills echoes of the ancient war-booms of Powys.

Today Powys is a Derelict Area, its wealth syphoned off to England, its industries shadows of their old selves. The Struggle goes on.

YOU ARE NEEDED FOR IT!

June — July, 1956

CYMRU, CYMRU UWCH YR HOLLFYD!
(Cân wladgarol ar y dôn 'Awstria' gan Haydn)

Cymru, Cymru uwch yr hollfyd
Galw arnom mae yn awr!
Cymru, Cymru, gwlad ein mebyd,
Codwn fry ei henw mawr,
Yn y meysydd a'r coedwigoedd,
Ar y bryniau ban a'r môr,
Y cywirwn gamau'r oesoedd
O dan gadarn nawdd yr Iôr.

Awn i'r frwydr i waredu
Pethau gorau Cymru fad,
Hawl i feddwl a gweithredu,
Rhain fydd seiliau deddfau'n gwlad;
Ffurfiwn yma un Weriniaeth
Un wladwriaeth gyfiawn gref;
Un egwyddor ac un gyfraith
O dan wenau haul y Nef.

Adeiladwn ein Gweriniaeth
Ar y meini sicr hyn.

Amddiffynnwn ei thiriogaeth
Ym mhob cwm ac ar bob bryn,
O Lanelli i Drelawnyd
O Gaerwent hyd at Lechryd.
Cymru, Cymru, uwch yr hollfyd
Uwchlaw popeth yn y byd.

I.O. Ellis

BUILD THE NEW WALES NOW
ENGLAND'S GOVERNMENT OF DESTRUCTION MUST GO
by Mair Jones

One gets tired of the old, old story of proving and establishing the facts clearly that Wales is a nation. We have already proved our worth as a nation by our heritage, our character, our way of living, our National Institutions, Eisteddfodau, our literature and the history of our heroes and martyrs.

It does not seem honest to say and believe all these things about our nation and at the same time act as though the Welsh Nation were just a sentimental song in a Noson Lawen.

If we believe in our nation then it should be shown not only on the rugby and Eisteddfodau fields, but in all our daily lives, in all elections and in our political lives. Every nation has a duty to be true to itself first and then be a good neighbour to every other nation: "To thine own self be true, then canst thou not then be false to any man." That is the faith of true Nationalism. That faith is broken by the Welshman who leaves Wales for ambition, selfishness and personal gain. The true Nationalist strives to build a better country at home.

OUR NATIONAL HONOUR

If Government is to continue to treat us Welshmen as though we were merely a Western part of England, then that Government is not founded on truth. The society that men have built up here in the past hundreds of years in Wales is too important a thing to be ignored. **It is necessary to recognise Wales as a nation in order to recognise Welshmen as human beings with human rights.** The centralised government in London simply does not know that to destroy things in Wales is to degrade us as Welshmen and there are many who are helping to destroy what is Welsh in Wales betraying their own society. If we want the world to be a Society of nations, let us start by respecting and honouring the nation that is here on this very ground.

If we read back into the rich history of Wales we find fiery fearless men who would at a trumpet's call gather up arms to defend their land.

LOATHSOME LILIES

We are not of that character today, instead we have some loathsome so-called leaders in Wales. The policy of the lily white gloves will get no-where in the world in the present time.

The politics of a simmering stew of pacifism, sectarianism, teetotalism, chronic respectability and rag-bag nationalism is not the politics for Wales. We wait for the English to do things for us. We dare not accept responsibility for our own life in Wales. If another land will not help us then we must do things for ourselves. We cannot speak to other nations as equals unless we have our own Government. **Courage and will are unconquerable and can accomplish anything.** No Welsh Government would dare to suggest the eviction of families out of farms and the destroying of houses and land for afforestation, as was threatened at Rhandirmwyn.

10,000,000 gallons a day of Welsh water goes to English cities while we suffer drought, restrictions and industrial shut down. A Welsh Government would develop the water supply to the benefit of Wales.

NOW IS THE TIME

As it is, the English Government and the English Civil Service cares not two hoots for Welsh families, Welsh Society, old homes and their sacredness and the Annes of Wales.

How can they govern well what they do not understand?

Every nation has been called by God to be a blessing to mankind. He has given us a responsibility which we must exercise. **We must unite under one flag — Y Ddraig Goch — RAMPANT!**

A sacred trust lies on all Welshmen today in Wales to work for one end alone and that is Wales.

Today is the time to unite for independence, not in 2056.

Glorious Figures from Our Past . . .

JOHN FROST

Monmouthshire is in many ways the most typically Welsh of all the counties of Wales. Its leaders, from Cadwaladr the Martyr who died in battle against the Saxon, to Aneurin (still happily with us) have always been a headache to the enemies of Wales, but for sheer self-sacrificing determination and tireless idealism, none stands higher than **John Frost**, the shoemaker's son who became Mayor of Newport. From an early age he battled against the corruption of local politics and the dead hand of the great landlords. He spent more than one spell in jail and on one of these occasions used his enforced leisure to perfect his knowledge of Welsh. As a Chartist leader he successfully defied the Home Secretary, Lord John Russell, and achieved unparalleled popularity among his fellow citizens. He started a paper called "The Welshman" and poured out a stream of letters and pamphlets which were the terror of the corrupt in high places. When the great Welsh Rising of 1839 was first mooted in the hills and valleys of Monmouthshire, Frost was the obvious leader, and despite his personal misgivings he played an honourable part in that most honourable episode of the Welsh Fighting Century. He marched with the Army of the Valleys and shared their defeat. He underwent, with the other leaders, the ordeal of condemnation to death for High Treason will all the barbarous details demanded by English law. No longer young, he suffered all the indignities and cruelties of convict life on board a coffin ship and in the penal colony of Van Diemens Land. After sixteen years of hardship he was allowed to return to his daughter's home near Bristol, where he lived quietly for the rest of his long life, where he could look across the waters of the Severn Sea to the green hills of Gwent, in whose dark valleys his name remains to this day as an inspiration to the Welsh workers in the unending battle against alien exploitation.

YOU ARE NEEDED FOR IT!

August — September, 1956
Editorial:
REMEMBER AND BE PROUD
The Lessons of our National Struggle

In this year of 1956, Wales celebrated a number of significant anniversaries. First in point of time, it is *a century and a quarter* this summer since Lewis the Huntsman and Dic Penderyn rallied their men on the windy heights of Twyn-y-Waun, above Dowlais, and raised for the first time in our land, the Red Flag.

CENTURY OF BATTLE

A hundred years ago, while two working men of Pontypridd were writing our National Anthem (an occasion honoured by everybody except the Welsh B.B.C.), in far off Scotland the son of a humble family was taking his first look at the world. This was KEIR HARDIE, and it is to his memory, on the centenary of his birth that this number of the WELSH REPUBLICAN is dedicated. For the twentieth century opened with the grandsons of the men who had marched with Penderyn returning Keir Hardie to the English parliament. We recall this event in no spirit of mere sentiment, for the fact that the workers of Wales were the first to offer solid and sustained support to this great Scottish pioneer is of fundamental importance to the understanding of our present position. For since the beginning of the century, every anniversary has its own lesson.

Fifty years ago, after endless obstruction on the part of reactionary "workers leaders" Hardie at last succeeded in founding the Labour Party as we know it today (but not **quite** as we know it today, perhaps!).

THEY PAID THE PRICE

Forty years ago, with Hardie scarcely cold in his grave, broken hearted and betrayed, the manhood of Wales marched under their numb-skulled English generals to the bloody slaughter of Mametz Wood. But as the men of Tonypandy and Merthyr Tydfil rallied to the Union Jack and the British Empire, across the Irish Sea, Hardie's comrade, Jim Connolly, who alone stands as his equal, took the Irish Labour Movement with him in the proclamation of a free Republic, and met his death at the hands of an English murder-squad. But the lesson was not lost . . .

Thirty years ago, with the Welsh heroes paying the price of serving England's King and Country, there came a sudden stirring. Hardie and Penderyn lived again . . . for Nine Days . . .

Twenty years ago, the bitter price was still being paid, full measure, pressed down and over-flowing. But at dead of night Three Men went out and fired the huts of Penyberth, and a new spirit swept over Wales . . .

Ten years ago: the sky bright with "victory" and hope, the air thick with promises . . .

At every one of these decennial milestones we may pause and ask "What went wrong?" And yet, "though much is taken, much abides". Here and now, in 1956, there are those who will ask: Where is the Red Flag of Hardie and Penderyn? Where are the flames of Penyberth? As dead as the red roses that adorned Arthur Cook's button-hole in the Nine Days? The Welsh Republican Movement answers **NO!**

We believe that the re-alignment of thought and action which are being forced upon us by the pressure of events will justify the hopes and the visions of the old pioneers.

This number of our paper is largely devoted to Hardie's own writings. They can be read in some bitterness of spirit. Fifty years later, we still have the Ruritanian rubbish associated with Royalty, the paralyzing obstructionism generated by the Trades Union hierarchs, a subject and exploited Wales. But it is not in this spirit that we would have them read. As immutable as the Law given on Sinai, they stand awaiting fulfilment; neglected, "re-thought", forgotten and betrayed by the so-called "leaders" of today they yet point out the way we should go, and we neglect them at our peril. The Welsh people must, and will, rise to the challenge again, and declare our country a free Socialist Republic.

October — November, 1956
Editorial:

THE NIGHT OF THE FIRE

In this number of the WELSH REPUBLICAN, we take the opportunity of recalling yet another glorious anniversary. Twenty years ago this autumn, Three Men, in the name of Wales, fired the huts on an airfield at Penyberth, in Caernarfonshire, which was being built by the English government in defiance of the wishes of the Welsh people. Those three men were **Saunders Lewis, D.J. Williams and Lewis Valentine.** When apprehended, they defended themselves in court to such good effect that in order to secure a conviction the English were forced to move the trial to London, where a jury of alien cosmopolites sentenced these brave men to imprisonment and shame. The most conspicuous among them, Saunders Lewis, was disgracefully treated by the so-called University of Wales, and has only comparatively recently been accorded the academic acknowledgment to which his gifts entitle him.

At first glance, nothing distinguishes the action of 1936 more than its complete isolation from anything before or after it, both in the careers of the three protagonists, and in the movement of Welsh opinion in general.

The anniversary went uncommemorated in the paper published by the body of opinion which these men once led. The action nevertheless remains a tremendous uprush of archaic force, sweeping aside the mildewed weeds of academic respectability and white-gloved liberal hypocrisy. It was an action in the hidden and unrecorded tradition of our history, for when law and order offer no defence, the Welshman has never scrupled to use other methods. Our readers will be familiar with some of the highlights and some of the heroes in that endless battle, as we have chronicled them. All Welsh citizens will be familiar with events in an endless list of countries today, when the twilight of empires is the dawn of new hope for those bold enough to press their claims. Many will remember an occasion, four years ago, when the apathy of our country was shattered as unknown patriots attacked the Vron Aqueduct. Elsewhere in this issue, we focus attention once again on the Tryweryn Valley and the shameful fate that confronts it. We salute the men of 1936 as we saluted their predecessors — the men of 1831 and 1839, the quarrymen, the miners, the dockers, the farmers, all of whom have played their part in a glorious resistance. We salute them in confidence and pride that the Welsh of today will not be lesser men than their fathers.

December, 1956 — January, 1957
THE FRONTIER OF WALES

Our Special Correspondent discusses in this, the second of two articles, the important question of where the eastern land frontier of Wales lies. What territory will the Self-Governing Wales comprise?

BY MANAWYD (John Legonna)

Faced with the likelihood that those who will negotiate in the name of Wales will retreat from the Dee-Severn boundary this writer has recently undertaken a considerable reconnoitre of the frontier areas. It was a rewarding experience, and one to be advised upon every young patriot. Hazy concepts are swept away in the light of reality and one is rapidly brought to see what a piece of deceit and cowardice the acceptance of the thirteen-county boundary would involve.

The more I traversed the area the more I was touched by the living place-name evidence of our people's struggle for survival in past ages. I forgot "defensible ridges" and "dividing contours" and became absorbed in this living reality of our People's will-to-live.

Pentre Clem in North Shropshire can, surely, be no less Welsh than Pentre Galar in Carmarthenshire. Pentre Hodre in South Shropshire is surely as Welsh as Pentre Voelas in Denbighshire, and Pentre Jack in West Herefordshire as Welsh as Pentre Jack in Cardiganshire.

And how could Llandinabo near Ross-on-Wye be less a part of Wales than Llanbabo near Holyhead? And are not such names as 'Garth' and 'Kymin' in Gloucestershire typically and entirely Welsh?

Journeying through these areas incorporated by the English into England I became particularly aware of the vital, especial significance of every Welsh name. For here were the outposts, the sentry-boxes in the dire struggle of our People to be and to remain Welsh. Here were the districts where this struggle was keenest and the English will to subdue and eject most rampant and bitter.

Indeed of all places it is these places and these names which are most valuable to us in that here is enshrined the utmost of the virility and courage of our People in the defence of our nationality and our existence.

Wandering through Garaniw and Bettws-y-crwyn and Porthywaun it seemed inconceivable that the People of Wales could ever agree to have them wrenched permanently by the English out of the body of Wales. A thirteen-county boundary will leave these places and dozens of their like in England and will be a treachery against which every possible protest must be raised.

Let us examine the thirteen-county boundary in greater detail:

a) **The Oswestry salient.** A minimum line to incorporate this Welsh territory would pass through Welshampton, Ellesmere, Whittington, Knockin, Kinnerly and Pentre.

b) **The Chirbury salient.** Though well anglicised this smaller finger pointing into Montgomeryshire might fairly be crossed at Westbury and Worthen.

c) **The Clun salient.** This is part of an extensive hilly area stretching from Montgomery-Radnor right to the Severn. The Welsh area here is bounded by Bishops Castle and the rivers Kemp, Clun and Teme.

d) **West Herefordshire.** A minimum boundary here should pass from Knighton through Lingen to Presteigne and down the river Wye through

Kington and Eardisley.

e) **South Herefordshire.** The Wye to the minimum boundary from Eardisley to the Bristol Channel.

The following, therefore, represents the line behind which there must be no retreat:

Queensferry, Chester, Holt, Whitchurch, Ellesmere, Whittington, Knockin, Pentre, Westbury, Worthen, Bishops Castle, Leintwardine, Lingen, Kington, Eardisley, Hereford, Ross-on-Wye, Monmouth, Chepstow.

The struggle for Self-Government has certain corollaries, of which a small number must be considered crucial. One such corollary concerns the boundaries of Wales. It is as follows:

The more the People of Wales strive to make our country Self-Governing the more do they assert the nation's right to possess the Welsh National Territory in the entirety of its bounds.

By this assertion the People of Wales deny that the nation's boundaries have been determined for all time by the capricious motives of buffoons and apostates lording it in the wake of the defeat of Owain Glyndŵr.

And by the same assertion notice is brought to all whom it may concern that there is a responsibility imperative upon every Welshman negotiating in the name of Wales to ensure that a Self-Governing Wales shall possess a territory which conforms to the needs of the national environment and worthily commemorates the heroic struggle of our forefathers in the cause of the Nation's survival.

February — March, 1957

Editorial:

A few months before his death, Dyfnallt stood before a great crowd who had gathered in the mountains of Brecnock to witness the unveiling of a new and worthy memorial to Prince Llywelyn. In the blazing heat of a rare summer's day, with the breeze playing in his white hair, this noble veteran spoke words: "yn wyneb haul, llygad goleuni", which we commend to our readers:

OUR DUTY

"In these days of propaganda it is the duty of every Welshman to shout from the rooftops that WALES IS A NATION.

"It should be an axiom of our faith. Wales is our mother. We are not spectators, but her children, her sons and daughters. Being members rather than parts of a nation, we love her, not as a thing of propriety, but as a thing of beauty and a joy forever. What is a nation? Not a mere collection of individuals, large or small. London's ten million does not constitute a nation.

Nationality is the spirit which makes all men citizens, which knits them together for the common weal. Nationality is the atmosphere and environment of a distinctive people. It may survive without political autonomy, but no nation can work out its complete salvation without a body politic. The right of Wales to be called a nation cannot be questioned. The eternal essentials of nationhood are here.

CRITICAL TIMES

We are passing through critical times as a people. There are disintegrating forces at work in our midst. Some of them seem to be the will of an evil genius behind the scene, actuated by one purpose: the suppression of our very existence, others are the results of tendencies in modern life."

Dyfnallt enumerated some of these factors:
"the system of education dumped on us 80 years ago; the loss of 250,000 of our people; the decline in rural life, and the growth of 'Regional' ideas in the new reconstruction schemes. "Wales," he said, "is **one**, in the highest sense. The New Wales will realize its highest aspirations as a **whole**, as a **unit**. Today has its challenge to us all, a challenge to the whole nation. Are we to be submerged under the flood of alien forces and deadened by apathy, or shall we rise to the occasion as Welshmen proud of our great heritage? The soul of the genius and culture of our race must not just survive in the mountains of Wales; it must come out into the open, declaring its faith and summoning every atom of energy in its being, to outlive material forces which endanger its existence."

SHAME THE HACKS

Here spoke an old and honourable man, who must have known that he did not have long to live, who spoke the truth of his heart as if he already stood in the presence of his Maker.

What are the mouthings of the grubby hacks of the capitalist press compared to this? What are the bleatings of the fainthearts and the effeminate sneers of those who are proud to call themselves traitors? Let the apparatchik and the apostate dare their worst. If one old man can put them all to shame, what cannot a vigorous and united nation accomplish?

★ ★ ★

DYFNALLT

Bu farw Dyfnallt ddechrau mis Ionawr, 1957. Aeth ei lwch i ganol y gwynt a'r glaw ar Fynydd y Gwrhyd, ac erys bwlch ar ei ôl.

Y dyddiau hyn, ceir 'grant' i bawb, bron, a gais addysg. Yn ei amser ef, nid oedd ond gwaith dan ddaear nes i aberth ei gyd-lowyr, a'i astudio caled ei hun, ei ddwyn o'r pwll i'r pulpud, ac i'w Orsedd.

Pregethwr, gwleidydd, darlithydd, bardd, llenor, eisteddfodwr, golygydd,

Archdderwydd, ni bu Dyfnallt yn grintach â'i ddawn. Bu'n ben ar ei bobl am iddo fod iddynt yn bont.

Od oedd darllen am ei farw yn y wasg Saesneg, heb weld dim sôn am ei waith dros Hunan-lywodraeth i Gymru. Ychydig yn wir a gefnogodd yr achos mor gyson a mor huawdl.

Aeth Dyfnallt yntau o'n plith, i ddilyn y cewri eraill a'n gadawodd. T. Gwynn Jones, W.J. Gruffydd, Ambrose Bebb . . . ac yn awr Dyfnallt. Pwy sy'n codi i lenwi eu lle? H.D.

April — May, 1957

Glorious Figures from our Past . . .

EMRYS AP IWAN

Some of the greatest preachers of 19th Century Wales were not concerned with social struggle. The Kingdom preached by John Jones, Talysarn was 'not of this world'. John Elias again, was so much taken up with preparation for the hereafter that he reacted against progress 'here below'. Others preached differently. The social injustice they saw around them spurred them into the van of the people's struggles. Morgan John Rhys, forced to emigrate to America. Gwilym Hiraethog, friend of Mazzini and Kossuth, David Rees, outspoken editor of the 'Diwygiwr', Morgan Howells, brother-in-law of Dic Penderyn, such men fought worthily for the rights of the Welsh People. Of this stamp was the scholarly preacher and critic, EMRYS AP IWAN. His name will live for all time for his contribution to Welsh literary criticism, and his prose works, but he was a fearless champion in more active causes. For many years his ordination as a Minister was banned because of his fight against those who would have anglicized Welsh non-conformity. He called for a Welsh Parliament and was the first to show the way in which the Home Rule movement at the end of the last century was being led astray by over-emphasis on the 'sectarian' aim of Disestablishment. In his writing and preaching he brought the works of the great social and religious thinkers of Europe direct to the Welsh people, while those who decried him could think only through English minds. A man of great independence of spirit and thought, fine scholar, linguist, patriot, minister to the religious and social needs of his people, such was Emrys ap Iwan. In the mighty upsurge of Welsh democracy in the 19th Century, leading on to the twin aims of National Independence and social justice, Emrys ap Iwan was a vital figure. His keen insight and devastating logic cut through the tangled growths of alien authority and privilege, strengthened though they were by native ignorance and hypocrisy. The fight for Independence and Social Justice is still on.

YOU ARE NEEDED FOR IT!

Forge the WELSH FUTURE and inherit the glory of the WELSH PAST by joining the WELSH REPUBLICAN MOVEMENT.

* * *

August — September 1973

THE NEWS THEY DON'T PRINT
GELIGNITE AT MUSEUM

The National Museum of Wales in Cardiff; which perpetuates the shame of the Welsh nation, by having on permanent display, albeit in a thick bullet-proof case which is under constant guard, the Investiture Regalia of the Anglo/German Prince of Wales, received a nasty shock recently.

Found resting against the cabinet displaying the Investiture robes and baubles was a package containing 4 sticks of gelignite. The authorities were so shocked at this penetration of their security that they attempted to hush the matter up; thus the incident received no coverage in the newspapers or T.V.

It is obvious that the intrepid saboteurs were by this act serving notice on the Museum Authorities to remove the wretched feudal objects or else.

WELSH HERO
by The Editor

The imprisonment of Ffred Ffransis for 12 months at Huddersfield Crown Court last month, was a contemptible and savage act, typical of the actions of English Courts towards Wales over many years. Judge Colin Chapman, who sentenced Ffred, not only demonstrated a complete lack of any knowledge of the situation in Wales but arrogantly indulged himself in a scabrous bellicosity which indicates that he is a person totally unfit to sit as a judge in any court of law.

Those of us who know Ffred Ffransis, will know that he is not the sort of person who would ever want to escape the consequences of his actions, but in this instance Ffred did not even have a fair trial or a just sentence.

The campaign for a Welsh Broadcasting Service, in which Ffred has been in the forefront of for the past 3 years, is now supported by all major sections of Welsh life, as the National Conference of Broadcasting called by the Lord Mayor of Cardiff, last month, clearly indicates. In the light of this Ffred Ffransis, who was given 2 years imprisonment in 1971, in the early days of the campaign and whose heroic example has brought success a strong probability, should not at this time be locked up in an English jail.

Ffred is one of the great heroes of Welsh Nationhood, an outstanding example to us all; modest, kindly and humorous in personality, he lives a life totally dedicated to Wales. All Welshmen, worthy of the name, will want now to register their protest at Ffred's treatment; let us demonstrate together in the name of Wales and of moral justice our solidarity with Ffred and demand that he should be released.

REPUBLICANS OF CYMRU

An object lesson in the exercise of political discipline was provided by the way in which the English ruling class, after destroying the Crown's power of direct rule, continued to use the myth of their own subject status to help maintain authority so effectively in their own country and to impose it upon so many other nations of the world. What, for instance, could have been more calculated to keep 'native' populations in a state of respectful awe and obedience than to see the great white lords themselves in their beplumed splendour bowing low before the visiting rahj.

By this second half of the 20th century, of course, the ruling class of England is as likely as not — depending upon the electoral whims of the English population — to be based upon a wider representation than formerly. But whatever vagary — Tory — Labour — Labour — Tory — the Westminster governmental succession may follow, it continues with the monarchy at its service to be used like a conjuring trick, as it were, to mesmerize and thus to govern other peoples.

It was in this tradition and for that purpose that the two royal ceremonials were staged in Caernarfon this century, bringing greater shame on our nation than the tricks and terror of the conquering English king in the 13th century. Our humiliation was compounded and perpetuated with the collaboration of a section of our own people. And Cymru — the first nation to suffer the English imperial ploy — remains one of the nations still suffering it.

To rescue us from this lower-than-colonial status of degradation, this elimination from the political map of the world via the English statute-book we must re-establish our national self-respect. The word self-respect in this context had long become a platitude in our mouths. But by today, mainly through the endeavours of Cymdeithas yr Iaith, that platitude is being clothed in dignity and meaning. When that same will to self-respect is as insistent on one side of the language demarcation line as the other then we shall be the proud possessors of a national movement of irresistible strength.

It goes without saying that it is not mainly around the language in the first instance that we can expect the will to national self-respect of our young non-Welsh speaking people to gather inspiration and purpose. Material considerations, such as, for instance, a deteriorating economic situation can be factors contributing towards the resurrection of a people's self-respect. But it is not enough for us to wait for time and the flow of events to bring us our chances. We ourselves by the power of our will and our political imagination must create our own conditions in this time of crisis for nation and language and the need for nation-wide support for those already deeply committed to the fight. There is need for a compelling political concept to create in the minds of our young non-Welsh-speaking a consciousness of national identity and distinctiveness corresponding to that which motivates their Welsh-speaking fellow Cymry and which will bring them together to go on side by side.

There is no other people in the world for whom the republican form of government would be more happily appropriate than for us the Cymry. There is a substantial body of republican-minded people in our country. Now is the time for such self-respecting Welsh men and women — without any need for infringing party loyalties — to make their republican presence unmistakeably felt in their effort to stir the apathetic ones of our young people from their apathy.

C.B.